MY SECRET CHILDHOOD

growing up in New York

To Kate,
Robert DeMaria

by the same author

CARNIVAL OF ANGELS
CLODIA
DON JUAN IN LOURDES
THE SATYR
THE DECLINE AND FALL OF AMERICA
TO BE A KING
SONS AND BROTHERS
SECRET PLACES
THE WHITE ROAD

MY SECRET CHILDHOOD

growing up in New York

by

Robert DeMaria

The Vineyard Press, Ltd.
Port Jefferson, NY

first edition

The Vineyard Press, Ltd.
106 Vineyard Place
Port Jefferson, NY 11777

ISBN: 1-930067-42-9

COVER: early family photo of the author taken on
the rooftop of a tenement house in East Harlem
about 1932

1

The First Revelation

I know now that it was probably March and that I was about three and a half years old. I was a blackboard on which something I did not understand was being written.

The sun had been shining the day before. Now the wind was blowing and the sky was thick with clouds. "Go down stairs, but stay by the house," my mother had said. "Don't go in the street and don't go up the stairs to the El. If it rains, sit in the hallway until I come down."

My father had been standing by the window. He was tall and silent and angry. When he turned around he caught me with his deeply shadowed eyes. The fields of white were rimmed in red. He wore a wrinkled jacket and a white shirt that had not been washed for a long time. His face was unshaven. He frowned as though it were difficult for him to see me. The light was behind him, and the sound of the approaching train rattled the window.

Once he had broken a window, and my mother had screamed. I could not say when because I had not yet solved the mystery of time. I was in the next room but there were no doors in the three room, cold-water flat. I buried my face in the pillow, too frightened to cry, breathless and beyond tears, my small fists clenched, my heart pounding, my mouth dry. The darkness was a blanket that smelled of the dampness, under which there was a rubber sheet. I had wet the bed again.

The voices of my parents became a dream that

1

returned often and was always the same, but the day I was sent downstairs to wait on the stoop for my mother was not a dream. She kissed me, and nudged me out. "Be a good boy," she said. "Maybe we'll have something to eat tonight."

There had been other apartments. When we could not pay the rent we were *dispossessed*. The very word frightened me long before I knew what it meant. We stood on the sidewalk. My mother cried. Somebody passed a hat, and a man with a pushcart took our furniture and cardboard boxes to another empty apartment a block or two away. The deposit was two dollars, and the rent was about ten or twelve dollars a month.

This time we lived one flight up on Second Avenue and the train went by our uncurtained living room windows. I could hear it long before it arrived, a monster rocking along with lights for eyes. The wheels of the train made a slicing sound and then screeched as the heavy machine came to a stop at the elevated station at 111th Street. When the lights in the train were on, I could see the people, men in dark fedoras and women in cloth coats, sometimes trimmed with the fur and mask of a dead fox. If they saw me at all, their glances were blank, as if they were too tired to distinguish between me and the red-brick facade of the tenement house. I would be sitting on the wide window sill, my knees pulled up to my chin. If it was a rainy day, I would spend it all on that window sill, watching the drops of water slide down the glass in an endless variety of ways. I turned them into racing cars or people and invested my hope in the destiny of one or another of those beads of moisture. It was a drama with hidden excitements that I never shared with anyone. It was

2

mine, and as long as no one knew about it, it could not be taken away from me.

My sister, who was almost five, sat on the day bed and talked to her doll, whose head I had once removed and then replaced, after which it was never able to cry again. My brother, who was two years younger than I, spent most of his time hanging over the side of his crib and picking plaster from the damaged wall. We laughed when he ate it and then told our mother. We were hoping that she would spank him, but she didn't. He was the baby.

"And don't talk to anyone," my father had said as I looked back from the open door. I was glad to be going, but it was a dark hallway with a long flight of wooden steps before I reached the daylight of the front door of the old tenement house. The stoop had two cement steps and cast iron railings. I did not know at the time what my parents were doing or why I was sent away.

I looked up through the girderwork of the El. It almost blocked out the sky. Under the tracks there were cars and trucks and trolleys. I sat on the stoop and watched them go by. The light was fractured into patterns of shade that animated the traffic on the street. Sometimes there was a peddler's wagon drawn by a tired horse with blinders and metal shoes that clip-clopped on the cobbles with the regularity of a great clock -- a sad sound.

I sat there for a long time, trying to remember the things I was not supposed to do. I wore short pants and woolen socks that came up to my knees. They did not keep out the chill. The day before, the sun had been out all day and my mother had said, "It's almost spring." For a moment she smiled and shaded her eyes to look at the sky, but soon she looked sad again. "I think he's coming home tonight," she said, meaning my father. "Maybe he'll bring something for you." She did not try to explain how he worked or where and why they always seemed to be fighting when he was there. It was years before I understood about his drinking, about prohibition and the places where he stopped and the the friends he had. "When we lived downtown, he was a different man," she said, as if she wished she had a grownup to talk to. "If it wasn't for those friends, the ones he met in the navy..." She stopped herself.

I stood up to button my sweater and pull my knitted hat down over my ears. Then I climbed one of the railings and straddled it like a horse, but it hurt my bottom and I climbed down again. There was nobody to play with. I didn't know anyone except my brother and sister. I sat down again and watched the people who walked by, but what I saw was mostly their feet and legs. Some of the shoes were nice. I found a pointed piece of wood and dug the dirt out of the cracks in the sidewalk. That didn't lead to anything, so I went to the curb and dropped the stick in the trickle of dirty water in the gutter that I imagined was a river. I was very high up somewhere and looking down. The stick washed away along with shreds of horse manure and cigarette butts.

Next to my house there was a brick wall with pieces of paper stuck on it. There was the face of a man with a smile and a big chin. I could not have known that his name was Roosevelt and that he wanted to be president. I was much more interested in the circus poster, the ferocious tiger and the man with the whip.

Next to the wall of pictures there was a store with candy and toys in the window. When someone gave us a penny we would go there. I looked at the small metal cars and the cowboy guns in holsters. There were cobwebs inside the window and a cat who slept curled up so that I could not see his eyes. One of the guns was a miniature six-shooter with a handle made of wood or bone. I had never been to the movies and I could not read, but I had seen pictures of cowboys in magazines and coloring books. I wasn't exactly sure what a gun was, but I liked the look of it and of the belt and holster. What I knew in those days came to me through instinct or revelation and was accompanied by a strange feeling of guilt and echoes of my mother's voice: "Don't go away from the house. Don't go in the street. Don't go up the stairway of the El."

I walked back to the building we called our house, paused for a moment and then walked further on to where the staircase to the station began. I looked up. There were many steps, then a landing, and then more steps. There was a thrill of fear in my stomach, as though my father had thrown me in the air and might not catch me.

The minute I set foot on the first step it occurred to me that my parents would know what I was doing. How could they not know? A little cloud of doubt and curiosity made me me bold. I looked around and then went up another step. I stopped on the landing and looked back. I was shocked by the height I had achieved by going up those stairs, and frightened by my disobedience. If I had been able to speak it I might have said, "Why is this a forbidden place?" And when I saw other people go by me, some of them holding children by the hand, I wondered why they could go where I could not.

I stayed on the landing, unable to go any further and unable to go back. There was a wooden barrier that kept

5

the wind out. I sat down and leaned against it. My stomach made its usual sounds and I became aware of my hunger. There had only been a slice of bread in milk that morning -- free milk from the bottom of the tank at Mr. Katz's grocery store and bread from the school, where we had to go first thing in the morning and wait in line.

I became aware of something else as I sat there -- I had to pee. It was like being in bed, except that I could not fall asleep and just do it without having to decide between the darkness of the long hall and the wetness of the sheets. I hugged my knees and rocked back and forth against the torn picture on the wooden barrier. All that remained of the picture was one side of a woman's face and her slender arm. She was probably beautiful but the dagger shapes in the ripped paper suggested violence and I kept turning to look at her over my shoulder to see if she was still there. I tried bumping my legs together to keep from wetting myself. Suddenly, a train arrived and a group of people descended the stairs, clutching pocketbooks, newspapers, and shopping bags. They seemed to be in a hurry and their feet made sharp and shuffling sounds. I stood up and tried to look invisible. A few people noticed me, some of them annoyed, some with a kind nod. One man in a black hat leaned over and said, "Where do you live sonny? Are you lost?" I shook my head and pointed to the nearest building. "Well, you better go home little man. It looks like rain and your mother will be worried." I nodded my head and he went on his way. In a few minutes the platform was empty again and the train was gone.

I looked through the railings and down to the sidewalk. I could do it there, I thought, and watch it go all the way down. Sometimes my mother would tell me to do

6

it from the curb into the street. I had even seen men doing it that way or maybe between two parked cars or against a wooden fence. I thought about going home in spite of what my mother had said. Perhaps I could do it in the dark hallway without anyone seeing me. And then, suddenly, it happened, as if the distant rumble of the next train brought it on along with a cold chill at the back of my neck. I sat down and hugged my legs but it was no use. And then, as the crowd came down again, I tried to look innocent, which wasn't easy, sitting in a puddle of my own pee. "You poor child," said a woman with very red lips. She pressed a coin into my hand and closed it for me. I don't know why I held it out. Perhaps as an explanation, though I was perfectly able to talk. "He's very smart," my mother had said to a friend one day as we stood in line at the school. "He didn't talk until he was two, and then, suddenly, out came these whole sentences and every word perfectly pronounced. But he's shy. He won't talk to just anyone."

I put the coin in the pocket of my sweater and held out my hand again. A woman put a penny in it and the woman behind her matched it with another penny. The next time I put out my hand I said, "Penny?" It worked. Suddenly, life was very wonderful and interesting. I spoke up a little more boldly and soon I had several nickels and two dimes as well as the pennies. When I finally descended the stairs, it was not with a sense of shame or guilt but with a feeling of triumph and the conviction that people were good and were giving me money because I also was good, even if my pants were wet.

I took my treasure directly to the candy store and bought a cowboy gun and holster on a belt that held six little wooden bullets. Does your mother know you're here?

said the man. I nodded without looking up at him. You're two pennies short, but that's all right, kid. Now go right home. I'll watch you from the door. And he did, all the way until I went into the dark hallway of our building.

The stairs squeaked. I paused to look out the only window at an air shaft, at the bottom of which there was decaying garbage. I went on up and listened at our door, but there were no voices. At the end of the long hallway there was a bathroom, the only one for four apartments. When I had to go, my mother took me, and each time she said, "There's nothing to be afraid of, dear." I didn't believe her, but I could not name the monsters that I knew lurked there. In one of the other apartments there was an old man without teeth who wore suspenders. He shuffled down the hall in his slippers, mumbling all the way to the bathroom. Maybe I would kill him with my new gun, I thought, feeling for the bone handle.

I went into our apartment and found my mother breaking up a wooden box for the potbelly stove in the kitchen. The pipe went out the window where there would have been a pane of glass and up the airshaft. A single bulb dangled from the ceiling. "I was just coming down to get you," she said. "I didn't forget." When she saw the new gun and holster, her face turned pale. "What's that?" she said. "Where did you get that?"

I told her what happened. "Oh, my god," she whispered, putting her finger to her lips as a warning. "Your father's going to be angry when he sees that."

"When I see what?" said the man who emerged from the shadows of the bedroom. He was a handsome man, not yet thirty, somewhere between lean and gaunt. I had seen a picture of him in his navy uniform. He was sitting beside my mother on a fake boat called the Coney Island. Now his eyes were puffy and his hair was uncombed and uncut. "What's going on here?" he said. "Where have you been?" He frowned when he saw the toy gun. "Where did you get that?" he said, raising his voice. "Come here, you little thief!"

I froze, terrified. My mother stepped forward protectively and tried to explain. "He was sitting on the steps of the El and some people passing by gave him a few pennies. He didn't know any better. We'll just take it back."

"You're damn right we'll take it back. I won't have anyone in this family begging." He took me firmly by the arms and knelt down on one knee to confront me. "Did you ask for money?" he said in a loud voice. I couldn't speak, and in the next moment I saw my father's hand flash across my field of vision. I felt it against my cheek and the side of my head. It seemed immense and heavy -- the hand of a coloring-book giant. I fell backward against the stove and then to the floor, too quickly to be burned, but wounded in a way that would last forever. He had held my hand and bought me ice cream in Central Park, and now he was tugging at my belt and removing the gun and holster.

My mother picked me up and held me against her thigh. "He's all right," my father said. "I'll bring this back to the store and give that guy a piece of my mind."

"Will you bring back the money?" she said.

"I'll be back later," he said. "Your aunt is coming over and I don't want to be here."

She knew it was pointless to argue with him. She was silent until he was gone, and then she sat down at the kitchen table and said, more to herself than to me, "What are we going to do?"

I shrugged my shoulders and went into the living room to sit by the window. I could hear my brother crying in the bedroom. My sister came out of hiding and said to me, "You shouldn't have done that. It's bad to take money from strangers."

"Why?" I said.

She thought about it for a moment and then she went into the kitchen to ask my mother. At the same time someone came to the door. It was my mother's Aunt Marta, who always wore black and always said the same things: "I can't give you any money, because he will take it and drink it away. And if you don't give it to him he will beat you. God forgive me for saying it, but you would be better off if he was dead. Then the government would give you a little something. Until then, I don't know what you can do." From her shopping bag she took a few things and put them on the table.

My mind drifted away to the outside world, where it had begun to rain. In that moment, in that very moment, something strange happened, and I understood it, not in a learned language, but in the script of heartbeats and the deep logic of the life force. I saw a piece of the sky beyond the ghostly station, and I looked down the long track that disappeared into the mist. Sitting by that window in East Harlem, with no knowledge of geography or history, and with no weapons except rage and secrecy, I decided to conquer the world.

2

The Second Revelation

I learned about death too soon. There were dead pigeons in the park and on the roof of our building, where a man with a long pole made them fly. There were dead rats in the street and in the back yard, killed by the fearless, scarfaced cats of the local alleys.

I killed flies with a flat stick from an orange crate. We went to the open market under the railroad overpass on Park Avenue to look for wooden boxes and overripe fruit in the garbage bins. Don't tell anyone, my mother said one day, as if I could understand the subtle issues involved in food-gathering.

I studied flies and the horses that provided them with food. The horses pulled the wagons of the unshaven peddlers who called out their wares: "I got on-ions here! I got pota-toes!" Women watched at their windows for them and then went down to the street with their shopping bags.

I killed lots of flies without remorse and saw an occasional dead cat in the back yard, but in the hot summer of 1932 I saw a horse drop dead in the street. He made a terrifying thud and overturned a wagon full of watermelons. The Italian peddler cursed at the horse and at the people who tried to pick up his watermelons. Then he wept and sat down on the curb in despair. I saw the glass eyes and the stillness of the horse and heard the whispers of the crowd that gathered there. The sparrows who feasted on a nearby heap of manure seemed unaware of the death of their host.

Strange weeds began to appear in the garden of my childhood. I saw a man with no legs, pushing himself along the sidewalk on a small board with skate wheels. He used a pair of small flatirons to shove himself forward, and he wore a pair of old leather gloves from which the fingertips had been cut. In an apron around his waist there were yellow pencils, and around his neck a tin cup on a string. There were a lot of men with missing limbs, but no women. Later, I learned they had been soldiers in the Great War that ended in 1918, the year that the Spanish flu killed my maternal grandfather and millions of other people. He died young, ten years before I was born.

Until I was almost four years old, I was immortal. Then I was plunged into the dark heat and confusion of scarlet fever. One night I woke up sweating and shivering and unable to breathe. I tried to call out but could make no sound, as though I were trapped in a strangling silence. My bed became a boat that rose and fell in a violent sea. The walls leaned towards me. I tried to get up but I kept falling backward and into vivid nightmares, in which bells and sirens were ringing and monsters hovered over me. I heard my mother's voice, but I could not see her. I was being wrapped in cold, wet sheets by two men in white. When I was helpless and strapped into the sheets, one of them carried me out of the apartment. I could feel him descending the stairs, and I could hear the heavy footsteps of several other people. "He's burning up," somebody said. "He's delirious." My head and face were covered. I thought of the Gypsies who lived around the corner in a store. "Stay away from them; they steal children," my mother's sister said. She lived with us for a while and slept on the floor.

She didn't like me because I was in the habit of breathing through my mouth. "What are you trying to do, catch flies?" she would say. "And when are you going to stop pissing in the bed?"

When we got to the street I could tell that it was dark, but I didn't understand what was happening. My head throbbed with pain. The metallic doors slammed shut. I was strapped to a narrow bed. Somewhere my mother was crying. A man in white said to her, "You'll have to keep away. It's very contagious. We have to take him to Communicable Diseases, downtown on the East River. The engine of the ambulance started up with a roar, the bells sounded and we drove off recklessly, lurching this way and that to avoid the posts that held up the Second Avenue El. The last thing I remember is that the world was upside down and that I was falling into the dark sky. By the time we reached the hospital I was unconscious.

I don't know how long it was before I was conscious again and aware of the clean sheets of the hospital bed and the wooden braces on my elbows that made it impossible for me to bend my arms. The nurse who leaned over me tried to explain that there were sores on my head and that I was not supposed to scratch them. Suddenly, I saw my parents and aunt behind a glass partition. Their mouths were moving, but I could not hear what they were saying. They made odd gestures and laughed.

The nurse showed me the bag of oranges they had sent. I couldn't believe that they were all for me. I loved oranges above all other fruits. And these were navel oranges, without seeds and easy to peel. I could imagine the cool juice in my dry mouth. The nurse prompted me by putting one of the oranges in my hands. My audience kept laughing and pointing as I tried, stiff-armed, to peel it. I begged the nurse with my eyes to remove the braces from my elbows, but all she said was, "Let me peel that for you." She had to pry the orange from my hands. "Don't worry, I'm not going to take it away." I watched her quick hands and noticed the fullness of her bosom and the stiffness of her white cap. She threw the peels away and tried to put a segment of the orange in my mouth. I shook my head. "I can do it," I said. She shrugged and then laughed with the others as I tried to figure out how to get the fruit into my mouth from a distance. I lay on my back with my arms straight up in the air. I took a piece of the fruit and let it fall towards my open mouth, as if I were bombing a small target. They were all amused when I missed and hit myself on the nose. I went on trying with such determination that eventually the nurse was moved and took off the braces. "But you have to promise not to scratch your head. Do you understand?" I agreed and stuck to my promise so scrupulously that I spent a night in agony, unable to ease the itching of those fever sores. I wet the bed, of course, but no one punished me.

When I got home from the hospital my cruel aunt said, "You nearly died."

My mother hushed her. "You'll be all right now," she said, touching my cheek and hair. Then she scolded her sister, who was younger than her. "Don't say things like that. He doesn't understand yet."

That night I could not sleep. What was the great mystery they knew but I did not? I heard my aunt's voice over and over in the darkness: "*You almost died.*" I thought of flies and cats and the dead horse and the suffocating heat and noise in the ambulance until a cold curtain came down and everything went dark and silent. I was afraid to go to sleep that night because I was afraid I might wet the bed and be sent back to the hospital to die.

I was still too young to know what it all meant, but soon my great-uncle would die, and I would get a little closer to the dreadful truth. He was the elderly husband of my mother's Aunt Emily.

I always liked visiting her. She lived in Greenwich Village, where we all had lived before my father decided to move uptown to the Italian neighborhood in East Harlem. She had an elegant house and a player piano on which the keys moved though no one was playing. While she and my mother talked and drank tea in a sitting room full of plants and rugs and framed portraits, I stared at the piano, determined to discover how it worked, and enchanted by the music. We had no radio or musical instruments.

Before he died, my great uncle had had a stroke and I can only remember him in that condition, an arm dangling, veins in his face, his lips quivering but silent. He sat in a carved wooden armchair, dressed in a fine suit, with starched collar and tie. Aunt Emily looked like the aristocrat she claimed to be. She was tall and slender with a lace collar that rose to her chin and a long dress that reached her ankles.

I am not sure that my mother told us that her uncle had died, but when she said we were going to Aunt Emily's house, I was all excited, because it meant a visit to the wonderful piano. When we arrived, however, we found the place full of people. It was the same living room, but this time there was something at one end -- something made of wood surrounded by a forest of flowers. Their fragrance filled the place, along with the smell of wool and perfume and coffee. Sounds and smells drifted in from a smaller parlor where some men smoked cigars and drank vermouth.

I desperately wanted someone to turn on the piano, but my mother leaned over and said, "You mustn't touch anything. You won't be able to listen to the piano today. There are too many people, and--" She stopped as if she did not know how to explain the occasion. She lowered her voice: "Uncle Adam is dead."

She wandered off and I found a place to hide between a potted palm and the piano. I secretly stroked the polished wood and tried to see behind it, but there was not enough light. I noticed that the people were all dressed in black and that some of them were speaking in a language that I did not understand. Eventually, my mother would explain to me that this part of the family had come to America from Italy about fifty years earlier in the 1880's, but, as a child, I never thought that this had anything to do with me.

I peeked out from behind the palm tree towards the flowers and the wooden box, which had brass handles and a silky lining. The people seemed to be moving in that direction. Women paused before the thing and lifted their veils. Men cleared their throats. My curiosity drew me out of hiding and I made my way along the wall, under a mirror, below a crucifix on which there was a man who was bleeding and nearly naked. Then I saw him. It was Uncle Adam. Or was it? He was lying very still in the silky interior of the beautiful box, as though he was sleeping. But I knew, instinctively, that it was not that simple. His face was chalky and there was lipstick on his lips. A woman leaned over to kiss him. She clutched a white handkerchief and kept making the sign of the cross. I was pushed forward by someone and found myself standing very close to the coffin. I froze with fear. "Kiss him. Kiss him," somebody urged. "He's going to heaven." It was a large woman in black. Before anything else could happen, my mother appeared and pulled me by the arm. "Don't go there," she said. "You don't have to see that." She led me into the smaller parlor and handed me a piece of cake. "Stay here. We'll be leaving soon," she said. I sat on a footstool and ate the cake. "Almonds!" said an old man in a black suit. "There are almonds in it." There was a smile on his face and yellow stains on his white moustache. I leaned away from him and his smile faded.

My father was often gone for days. He would wind up on the Bowery, where homeless alcoholics drank together and slept on pieces of cardboard in the hallways of unoccupied buildings, or even on the sidewalk, leaning against brick walls or garbage cans. When he came home he slept like a dead man on the day bed in the living room, and we were all told to be very quiet. My mother knew that when he woke up he would be desperate for a drink and might be sick or violent.

In the afternoon he woke up screaming something about machine guns on the wall. His eyes were wild, his face pale and gaunt. My mother came into the room wiping her hands on her apron. "I'll make you some coffee," she said. "I'll get some sugar from Anna next door." He reached for her in his panic, but she stepped away. He fell back onto the bed and began to tremble all

17

over as if he was naked in the snow. But outside it was spring and the sun was shining. By this time I was a year older and we had moved across the street to another apartment, which was no better than the last one. There was no linoleum on the floors. The electricity had been turned off, but the two-burner gas stove worked and the bathroom in the hall was nearby.

I sat on the floor and played with a few toys in a cardboard box, but I kept an eye on my father, who looked as though he might either explode or expire. After a while his shivering subsided into a rocking motion and he began to moan. My mother came back with a mug of coffee and made him sit up. She had a wash cloth, with which she tried to wash his face. I noticed that he was unshaven and that his face was bruised. "Did you fall down?" she said, but he didn't answer. She looked over her shoulder at me. "Go in the bedroom and play with your brother," she said.

From the bedroom I could hear my father get sick and I could hear them arguing. "You'll die if you go on like this," my mother said. "And I'll die if I quit," he said.

"But think about your family."

"Maybe I should just go away and stay away. I'm no good," he said.

There was a long pause. My sister came in from across the hall where she was playing with Anna's daughter. She stayed in the bedroom with me and my brother, and we waited while the light faded.

That night my father ate with us and looked much better, but in the morning he was gone.

The next time we heard from him he was in Bellevue Hospital with pneumonia. There was a phone booth in the candy store next to our building, and one day a

18

boy came up to our apartment and handed my mother a note that said she was supposed to call a certain number.

She took my sister and me with her and left the baby with Anna. We went downtown on the trolley, which was a great adventure. It was not just the traveling and the physical motion that I liked, but the trolley itself, its shape, the windows, the yellow wood. I insisted on sitting near the front on the stiff woven-straw seats, so that I could watch the conductor. He pushed the lever and a surge of energy moved the trolley forward, slowly at first and then faster. He pulled a cord and rang the bell. It was all wonderful.

I was so intrigued that a few days later, when I saw an electric Railway Express truck parked near our house, I got into it, my heart pounding, and played driver. I pushed the lever and the vehicle lurched forward. It went half a block before I pulled the lever back and it stopped. Somehow it managed to miss the parked cars along Second Avenue and the posts of the El. I was terrified and ran up to the roof to hide behind the pigeon coops. It was hours before they found me. Instead of scolding me, my mother hugged me. I didn't understand why. "Maybe he'll be a car thief when he grows up," said my aunt. When she laughed, she cackled and her gums showed. "The trouble with boys is that they grow up to be men, and all men are bastards." I later learned that she had had a boy child at the age of sixteen and had given it away to the father's family.

At the hospital we walked down a long corridor with waxed green linoleum on the floor and yellow walls. My mother carried a folded slip of paper on which directions were written. She stopped a nurse and showed it to her. In the hallway there were wheelchairs and benches

19

and charts on the wall of people without skin, so you could see everything inside. "Don't bring the children in," said the nurse. "Tell them to wait for you here on the bench. It won't be good for them to go in there." We were standing before a pair of large doors. My mother looked frightened and we could hardly hear her when she spoke.

We sat there for a long time, slipping and sliding on the floor and standing on the bench to look at the charts that revealed muscles and blood vessels and inner organs. "He has no dingaling," said my sister, using the word that our aunt had taught us. I looked at the strange creature and saw that she was right. My sister covered her mouth and giggled, but I just stared at the place where the genitals should have been.

When my mother finally returned through the double doors, she looked troubled and pale. Her eyes blinked nervously and there was a crumpled white handkerchief in her closed hand. She told us nothing about our father and we did not ask her any questions. "We've got to go home now," she said. She held my sister's hand and my sister held mine. We knew there was something wrong and that it was best to be silent.

When we were back in the apartment Anna came in with my brother and said, "How is he?"

"He has pneumonia," she said. "The doctor told me that the last time he was in the hospital it cost them over a thousand dollars to save his life and that they have a lot of others like him. He said he couldn't promise me anything but that they would do what they could." She used her handkerchief and turned away from us so that we would not see her crying.

"He'll be all right," said Anna. "He's young.

They'll feed him up a bit and he'll come back. You'll see. Come now, we'll have a cup of tea. And bring the kids over later for a bite to eat. Jim's down the river somewhere on the tugs and won't be home until tomorrow."

Every day for a week she called the hospital and she was told that he was showing signs of improvement. She began to believe that he would recover. She even went to church with her rosary beads, though she was too practical to be an honest believer. It was a Sunday when the boy showed up at the door and handed her a note. It said, "Call the hospital right away." She rushed downstairs to the candy store, leaving us alone in the apartment. I followed her, but hid inside the doorway to wait for her to come out of the candy store. After a while I heard someone screaming. It did not sound like my mother. Then I saw her running out of the store, her face wild. She collapsed to her knees on the sidewalk and started tearing at her clothes and wailing, "No! No! No!"

I moved further back into the shadows and watched as a stranger stopped to comfort her. He tried to help her up but she was hysterical. In another few minutes Anna appeared and the two of them got her to sit down on the stoop. I ran upstairs and found the door open. "What's the matter?" said my sister. "I don't know," I said, and we sat down on the day bed and tried to be very good.

Aunt Maria, who was permanently in mourning, came over the next day to talk to my mother. She shook her head. "What a cruel way to tell a woman that her husband is dead! What beasts these doctors are!"

They talked for a long time and Aunt Maria said, "There's no place for him in the family plot at Woodlawn.

21

He's not a Perella. He's been in the navy; maybe the government can bury him. What about his family in Florida, his sister, his mother? That poor woman. She just lost her husband, and now her son. I'll talk to Emalinda." Then she cooked for us and her husband came over with some wine.

Several days passed before the hospital called again, this time to ask what arrangements had been made, because the body had to be removed. If it wasn't removed soon, they would bury it in potter's field, where they buried criminals and people with no names. My mother appealed again to Aunt Maria, who said, "No, no, you mustn't let them do that. They buried Judas in a potter's field. Go to Aunt Emily. She has money." Eventually, there were several small donations and arrangements were made for a simple pine box and an unmarked grave.

All I remember is a small group of people standing around on the soft earth near a hole in the ground. Whatever they were saying or doing was all meaningless to me. There was grass and I wanted to run, but my mother held me firmly by the hand. It was spring, perhaps May. In July, my father would have been thirty years old, had he lived.

I watched them lower a crude pine box into the ground. I stopped squirming, but I still could not comprehend what this ritual was all about. Suddenly, a man took me by the arm and another man showed me a shovelful of earth. "Put some in," he said. I looked in the hole and at the shovel and the man's face. "Don't be afraid; just take some earth and put it in there. You are the son. You have to bury him." Someone took my hand and shoved it firmly into the cold, damp earth in the shovel. I was startled, but then I heard my mother's voice: "It's all right." I understood only that I should throw dirt in the hole; I didn't know why. I took some in two hands and threw it in. I heard the sound of it on the pine box. "More!" said the man holding the shovel. I took a bit more and threw it. "His hands are too small," someone said. "Let him touch the shovel." Someone put my hand on the wooden part and the man holding it let the earth slide off into the hole. The thud was much louder. When I looked around for my mother, I saw that two men were standing close to her, as if to keep her from falling. Perhaps they were her brothers. Michael was twenty-nine, Joseph was twenty-three, and my mother was twenty-seven.

3

The Ghost of My Father

Shortly after the death of my father I had to be taken to a clinic to be circumcised because I had a serious infection. My mother did her best to explain what it was all about, but I did not understand. It was summertime and I would not be five until September.

In the months following my father's death, nobody mentioned him and all the signs of his existence had been removed from the apartment. There were no shoes on the floor, no pictures on the wall, no clothing, no smell of smoke or alcohol. I dared not ask what happened to his things. My mother seemed fragile and sometimes lost in a dream. Perhaps he didn't have anything. Perhaps his life had dwindled down to nothing but hallucinations and pain. Everything he owned could probably have been stuffed into a paper shopping bag and dropped into the garbage bin. In time, my memory of him and those several months faded, leaving behind only a hint, the traces left in a photo album after the photos had been removed.

The only thing that remained was the mysterious *circumcision*, apparently required by the doctor who treated me for scarlet fever. I could never remember the operation itself, nor can I say where it was performed or by whom, but I will never forget the cruel laughter of my aunt and my first sight of the bandages. I must have been put to sleep. I did not become aware of my condition until we got home and I had to go to the bathroom. My mother bent over me to open the buttons on my short pants. Her sister was sitting at the kitchen table with a cup of tea in front of her. She knew how to read tea leaves and had been telling my mother's fortune. She paused to watch the unveiling. As my pants came apart and down I was shocked to see nothing but a lot of gauze and cotton and adhesive tape. My aunt suddenly howled: "They cut off your dingy. It's gone. That's what you get for sitting around all day with your mouth open."

"Don't listen to her," my mother said. "It's there, and it will be all right."

"I don't see it," I said, my faced flushed with fear, and tears forming in my eyes.

"They cut it off, you little bastard," said my aunt. "You must have been playing with it."

"No," I said, appealing again to my mother.

She looked too weary to be angry. "It'll be all right by tomorrow. It's just a small cut. As soon as it heals we can take the bandages off."

"I have to pee, I said, feeling the panic like a hand at my throat. "How can I do it? I can't do it."

"That's a lot of bandages for a little cut," said my aunt. "Maybe they took the whole thing off and turned him into a girl."

"Oh, for Christ's sake, shut up," my mother shouted. It was a rare moment of rage and I could see in my aunt's eyes that she was suddenly afraid of her older sister.

My mother got down on her knees and started to remove the bandages. "Let's see what they've done to you." There were some spots of blood in the cotton but the wound itself was not bleeding. "I told you it was all right," she said. "It's already beginning to heal. Come to the bathroom and we'll see if it still works."

It did, of course, and was only a little tender for a few days. "No worse than a scraped knee," my mother said, but I knew there was more to it than that. Was I being punished? Perhaps I had wished for my father's death as others had, but I also wanted him to be alive again.

A few days later it happened. He was alive and he came to visit me in the night. It must have been a dream, but I remember it as a real occurrence, complete with the smell of the dampness of his coat and his heavy breathing and cough.

My mother and sister slept together in the only bedroom. My brother's crib was in the same room. I slept on the daybed where my father used to lie for hours, staring at the ceiling. There were stains there in which I saw a parade of animals. I don't know what my father saw.

The night he came to visit me it was very warm, and I slept fitfully, as though I had a fever. I heard something in the kitchen. Then I saw a dim light that made the walls seem yellow. There was no door between the living room and the kitchen. From where I was lying I could see part of the wall over the washtub. A shadow appeared on the wall and seemed to be doing something in the sink. I had once seen my father urinate there.

The kitchen light went out and the shadow moved into the living room, where the dull light from a lamppost filtered through a drawn shade. I could hardly see the shadow or the person, whichever it was, but I could hear his breathing, and I could hear his footsteps coming closer. A chill went through my heart, as though I had been stabbed by a dagger of ice. When he spoke, his voice was like the rush of wind in a rainstorm. "You all wanted me to die. You betrayed me." I shook my head and pulled away until I felt the wall at my back. "Don't lie to me. I took you to the park. Don't you remember?"

In the park one day he had helped me up the steps of a slide. I had been full of doubts until he touched me with his large, reassuring hand and urged me forward.

"Look at me," he said. I did, but it was hard to see his features in the dark shadows. There were street noises, including the sound of the elevated subway. For a moment he seemed to be slipping into a kind of mist. "It wasn't my fault," he said. "It wasn't anybody's fault. Just bad luck." His voice weakened. "Think of me! Remember me!"

As he began to recede into the darkness I could hear myself call out "Pa," as if I were two people. He did not answer. In another moment he was gone and I could breathe again. I heard my mother approaching the living room. I knew the sound of her slippers on the linoleum. "Are you all right?" she said. I realized I was sitting up in bed and that I was wide awake. I felt confused. "Is your bed wet?"

"No," I said. I hesitated and then decided not to say anything further about anything. She kissed me on the forehead and, almost instantly, I fell asleep.

4

My New Life

Sometime between the death of my father in May and the beginning of Kindergarten in September we moved from Second Avenue and 111 Street to 112 Street between Third and Lexington. These things were arranged by the adult world, which now included an investigator from the Welfare Department of the City of New York. Our investigator was a Jewish woman of a certain girth, who carried her papers in a black briefcase. "I can see that you are a decent family," she often said, "but you wouldn't believe what some people do to get more money. They say their husband is dead or has deserted them. They borrow kids from their neighbors and claim that they were born in the apartment and weren't registered. At night they give back the kids, and the husband comes crawling out of the woodpile."

She would settle in at the kitchen table and ask my mother a lot of questions: "Are you pregnant? Did your kids get their diphtheria shots? Did you go to the clinic at Mount Sinai for your nervous condition?" My mother had not recovered fully from the shock of my father's death. Though she was strong and competent in some ways, she was fragile in other ways. She was thirteen when her father died in 1918. At fifteen she dropped out of high school to go to work for the Bell Telephone Company. At seventeen she had a nervous breakdown and her benevolent employer sent her to the country for a rest. Being a telephone

28

operator in those days was not easy. And now there was this tragedy. One day I heard the investigator say, "Perhaps we should place the children in a foster home for a few months so that you can recover from --"

"No," said my mother, squaring her shoulders defiantly. "I can manage."

The investigator looked over her glasses for a moment and then said, "I'm sure you can, Christina. I'm sure you can."

Our new apartment cost fifteen dollars a month and had three rooms. You had to go through each room to get to the next one. First came the kitchen, then the living room, then the bedroom. There was a toilet in the kitchen, and a washtub for laundry that doubled as a bathtub. The apartment was not much bigger than the last place we had on Second Avenue, but it was much lighter, because we were on the third floor and the building next door was a one-story garage. There was sunlight in the morning and a large tree in the back yard.

It was much better kept than any building we had lived in since we moved to East Harlem. The brass knobs and mailboxes were polished. The tiled floors were mopped regularly. The front door was locked and there was a buzzer system for visitors. The owner was a portly man with rimless glasses who lived in Queens and drove a new Buick. He had many apartment houses and an agent who collected the rent -- a bald man in a dark suit who did not like conversation and was always in a hurry. He directed ordinary complaints to the superintendent, who lived rent free on the ground floor with his wife and two kids. He was a Canadian named Croteau who worked as a sandhog in the new Lincoln tunnel. Sometimes he came home still wearing his yellow helmet with its single headlamp. I was very impressed. And when he got drunk and roared at everybody, I was even more impressed. I felt that we were all safe in a building that was guarded by such a broad-shouldered and fearless man.

Our neighborhood was a blend of many ethnic groups. To the east of us was the second largest Italian area in the city, and to the west of us was an early Puerto Rican settlement and then Black Harlem. The Methodist Church on Lexington Avenue and 111th Street had a congregation of mainly German-Americans. Across the street from our building there was a synogogue, and most of the pushcart peddlers in the Park Avenue market were Jews. Along Lexington Avenue there were quite a few Irishmen. Further north and east there was a small group of Russians and some Finns whose blond hair was almost white. There were still Italians on 112th Street, but they were moving East of Third Avenue. In our building we had French-Canadians, Czechoslovakians, Germans, Jews, and Italians. Within a few years the entire block would succumb to the Puerto Rican invasion, and the neighborhood would be called Spanish Harlem.

In the meantime, I was delighted with the little world of 157 East 112 Street. It was a time of discovery, a time of first things. I started school, I made my first friend, I was given my first book, I saw my first movie, heard a radio for the first time, and one day, my heart pounding, I was taken for a ride in the rumble seat of a Model A Ford owned by my uncle Charlie, who was known as "Babe."

My first friend was Alfred, a handsome boy who

30

lived across the hall from us. His hair was tightly curled and his skin was darker than mine. He said his father was an American Indian. One day my mother lowered her voice to tell a friend she thought he was a Negro, though his wife was white and spoke with a foreign accent. I preferred to believe Alfred and enjoyed listening to his made up stories about his father. We played cowboys and Indians in the back yard, where we built things out of stones and pieces of wood and poured water into rivers that we dug with sticks.

Alfred was an only child and had mastered the art of getting what he wanted. I made suggestions, but it was he who made the decisions about where we would play and when. I would knock on his door so gently that I was startled when someone answered. I had to learn everything about friendship. At first I didn't know what to say; I just presented myself, and his mother would smile and whisper: "Alfred's father is resting. Come back a little later." My mother explained that Mr. Alcorn did not like visitors.

Alfred had more toys than I did. Soldiers made of lead. Building blocks and coloring books and a wind-up train that ran in a figure eight on a track. One of my favorites was his dump truck. In the back yard we could load it up and transport toy-tons of earth and stone to build our trenches and forts for the great war that we were waging in our boyish minds.

In the summer, when there was no school and we were only six or seven, we played together all day, every day. At the time, I could not have imagined life without Alfred, but a few years later, with the neighborhood beginning to decline, the inevitable happened. Alfred's family moved away. They were just seven blocks further north, but it was not the same as being next door. I finally found the courage to venture up Third Avenue to find his new building, but when I got there I did not see him on the street and I was too shy to hunt for his apartment and knock on the door. Each block was like a separate village in those days. Strangers were noticed and could get into trouble. I hurried back to the safety of 112th Street.

At first I missed Alfred very much and retreated into the fortress of my inner life, where I was never bored. And then the widening circle of my universe began to include other children, some in the building and some in the local church, which my mother began to go to. She went because Helen and her family went. They were the Germans on the top floor: Helen, her husband, and their two daughters, one sweet and well behaved and the other full of the devil. It was the bad one who became my sister's best friend.

The school I went to was on 115th Street. I was only in kindergarten, but I thought it was wonderful -- a door that opened into another part of the larger world. It was here that I had my first graham crackers and drank milk from a small paper container. The simplest of things struck me as full of profound significance. I marveled at the immense wooden blocks, for instance. With a dozen of them, one could build a fort large enough to sit in, or make the outline of a pirate ship that could be completed in one's imagination.

From the very beginning I loved going to school, and from the first lessons in reading and writing in the first grade, I caught on to the whole notion of learning. Perhaps I had been given some practice at home or simply had a gift for language, but it seems to me I knew instantly and instinctively how to read and write. I listened for a few moments to a tale about a gingerbread boy and two stick figures named Dick and Jane. When it was my turn to repeat after the teacher, I simply read the whole mimeographed sheet and amazed the teacher and the rest of the class. "Where did you learn how to read?" said Miss Anderson.

I shrugged my shoulders. "I don't know," I said.

Soon after that I was given my first real book, *The Hardy Boys at Mystery Lake*. It had a hard cover and was not for coloring. It was the kind of book I saw for sale at the second-hand bookstore on Lexington Avenue. Though I found it difficult to read, it made me feel very grown up. It was given to me by someone we called Aunt Beatrice, a childhood friend of my mother's from Greenwich Village. She was a heavy woman with a nice smile, but, otherwise, not physically attractive enough to find a husband. She desperately wanted a child and treated me as though she were my mother. Before long she was visiting us every day and sometimes stayed overnight. I remember how she labored up those three flights of stairs, carelessly dressed, her shopping bags full of surprises.

In this period of first things I saw my first movie -- *Captain Blood* with Errol Flynn. My mother had been given some free passes by the Welfare Department investigator, Mrs. Feldman, who proved to be a helpful and friendly woman. She would sometimes stop by even when we were not on her schedule.

The movie was showing at the Loew's on 116th Street near Lenox Avenue. My mother got us cleaned and dressed and walked us there, making sure we all held hands. From the beginning it was a great adventure. I must have been seven or eight. My sister at nine was taller than me. My brother still wore his Buster Brown haircut.

Nothing could have prepared me for the miracle I saw that day. In a huge temple of plaster fountains and tapestries, with curved rows of seats for hundreds of witnesses, a giant version of reality was created on a screen. I would not have been surprised to hear that it was God behind the screen who made all of this happen.

I did not have to understand the plot to be awed by the pictures that moved and by the sounds. Voices roared and music drummed. History was beyond me and geography was an unexplored subject. I did not know what a foreign country was. I did not even know yet that I was from an Italian family or what that meant. None of this mattered when the battle scenes came. Men in strange costumes climbed into the rigging of old ships. Cannons exploded and fires raged. Naked swords glinted in the hot light of the flames. Men were slashed and stabbed and thrown into the sea. I shrank back in horror, prepared to duck beneath the rows of seats if any of the violence flew at me from the screen. The primitive science of a boy's mind was torn to shreds. This could not be happening in a dark arena with the sun shining outside and people going about their business. There had to be an explanation. There had to be!

My mother tried to provide it after we left the theater, but I was in a state of such feverish excitement that I couldn't understand what she was saying. A machine? Pictures? "Yes," she said. "The pictures are shown on the screen with a machine called a projector. Those things are not really happening. Were you afraid?"

"Yes," I said.

"I wasn't," said my sister.

"Me too," said my brother.

Though I finally understood the principle of the moving pictures, my life after that first exposure was never the same. I must have realized something about the power of the imagination and the uncertainty of reality. Someday those seedlings would sprout.

About a year later Uncle Joe gave us an old radio. He and Uncle Babe had opened a repair shop just east of Third Avenue on 112th Street. The radio was called an Edison Bell and looked like a miniature church. It did even more than the movies to make me aware of the world. I spent hours memorizing the stations and making a list of my favorite programs. There was fifteen minutes of news at 6:30 every evening, followed by Lowell Thomas at 6:45, *Amos and Andy* at 7:00, and *The Lone Ranger* at 7:30. In the daytime there were soap operas such as *Pepper Young's Family*, and there was always popular music, even an all-night program called *Milkman's Matinee*. For years, my sister and I battled for control of the tuning knob. I liked sports and adventure, and she liked Martin Block's *Make Believe Ballroom*.

Many new things were packed into those early years and remain unforgettable, but there was a note of sadness too, perhaps a shadow cast by the ghost of my father, who visited me in my dreams in many forms -- sometimes a tall man, kind and wise; sometimes a madman, a thief, or even a murderer. At times an invisible force, something far away but approaching like a runaway train or a tidal wave, or a monster inside of me, an imprisoned beast who might at any moment explode from my chest and be revealed.

5

The Affair of the Prune Box

At the age of nine I decided that I was old enough to earn some money. I studied the efforts of two boys on the block who had gone into the shoe-shining field. Patrick was an Irish kid who wore suspenders to hold up his knickers. When I asked him if he thought I was old enough to shine shoes, he gave me a contemptuous glance. "Nah!" he said. "There's black kids working all the good corners, especially by the subway stations, and even some men. They'll kick your ass. You have to know how to fight before you can shine shoes. And you have to know how to make a box and snap a rag."

The other kid was less discouraging. He was about fourteen, but he was short and had a young face, except that his jaw was peculiar. Some people called him Dino the Monkey. He wore long pants and a tight leather belt around his waist. The sleeves of his shirt were always rolled up high on his arms to make him look tough, but he wasn't. He had a soft voice and his eyes were always wandering up and down the block as though he were looking for someone. One Sunday I watched him shine Mr. Croteau's shoes on the stoop of our building. His beautifully made shoe-shine box was painted green, and there was a fancy foot rest screwed to the top of it. For a carrying strap he used an old belt that was given to him by his father. I wouldn't be able to get that, I thought, as I ran through a list of materials I might need to make a shoe-shine box as nice as his.

Afterwards, I walked down the block with him and watched him smoke a cigarette. "You're never too young to get started," he said. "How old are you, about ten or eleven?" I let him believe he was right. "I could teach you a thing or two."

"Like what?" I said.

"Like the best thing to use is a prune box. That's what I used."

"I never see anything like that in the market," I said.

"Of course not," he said. "Everybody wants them. I'll keep an eye open for one. but it might cost you a dollar, maybe two."

"That's a lot of money," I said.

He shrugged. We had reached Third Avenue. He looked uptown and then downtown. "Well," he said, "maybe we can work something out, like I can do you a favor if you do me a favor."

"Sure!" I said.

He smiled. "I'll look for you on the block."

"After school?"

"I don't go to school no more," he said. "I got better things to do." He glanced beyond me, still searching. "I'm going to head downtown, maybe 86th Street by the movies. Think about that prune box."

I didn't have to be told to think about it. I had already decided that it was the key to my new career and maybe my whole life. With a prune box I could make a shoe-shine box, and with a shoe-shine box I could make money. And if I saved enough money I could buy that old typewriter that Sidney Rothman had found in his father's cellar. My boyish plans for a future ended there in a kind of blind desire.

I walked back towards my building. It was Sunday and there was a big stickball game going on. The players were mostly Italians who played for money and cursed and argued about everything, saying your sister this and your mother that.

I sat on the steps of the synagogue and watched for a while. Somebody kept the score with white chalk on the street. I liked being there. I liked the game and the noise and the Sunday crowd and Mr. Croteau in his church suit and shined shoes, standing with some other men outside of a ground floor window where someone was tuned into the Yankee game on his radio. Then I heard two Italian guys near me talking. They had turned their heads simultaneously towards the corner of our street and Lexington Avenue, where three Puerto Ricans were standing, as if they were afraid to come any closer. "Fuckin' Spicks," said one of the Italians. "They're like cockroaches. Before you know it, they'll be all over the fuckin' place."

Monday was a good day to go to the market on Park Avenue. It ran for four or five blocks under the Grand Central overpass. Originally, it was just a gathering of pushcarts, but eventually the space was enclosed by the city and stalls were created that peddlers could rent. There were a lot of deliveries on Monday and, therefore, plenty of wooden boxes in the garbage bins, mostly orange and apple crates. There was a lot of competition for these boxes, because they could be broken up and used for firewood or they could be used for making things, like window boxes in the winter or wagons, if you had some old baby carriage wheels, or scooters, if you had some skate wheels. It was also possible to use the frames of the orange crates to make rubber-band guns that could shoot little squares of cardboard or even linoleum. If you had a hammer to get the nails out and a saw to cut up the wood, you could make almost anything.

I figured I would keep all that in mind, just in case Dino was unable to locate a prune box. The next time I saw him he had a bruise under his left eye. He said that his father had punched him and he was thinking about leaving home. "I'm tired of all of them," he said. "I'm the only one in the house who knows how to make some money. My old man don't like what I do."

"What do you do?" I said.

"Never mind what I do. Most of the time I shine shoes."

I paused and then pounced. "What about the prune box?"

"The what?" His frown made him look like Dino the Monkey.

My heart sank. "You know, for the shoe-shine box. I'm already saving up for the footrest and the other stuff."

"Oh, yeah, yeah," he said,"I asked around, but I can't find one yet. Maybe by next weekend."

On Sunday, I hung around the street all day waiting for him, but he never showed up. It never even occurred to me that anything in his life could be as important to him as that prune box. The day ended in clouds and drizzle and general disappointment.

On Monday afternoon I went to the market and managed to find an apple box. I took it home and got to

40

work in the back yard with the only tools I could find—an old hammer and a dull knife, which I stole from the kitchen. I had no idea where I could get a saw and no money with which to buy one. I imagined the knife might cut straight if I kept tapping it with the hammer. I was wrong. All I managed to do was to split the wood, which followed a very crooked grain. I did not give up. I kept cutting and banging and removing nails until I had a pile in front of me that looked depressingly like the firewood we used to put in the potbellied stove on Second Avenue.

I sat there alone in the dusk, glancing up occasionally at the laundry on the lines strung between windows and poles. Here and there a light went on and a shade went down. Some cats appeared, walking the narrow fences and looking curiously in my direction. Suddenly, there was a chill in the air and I knew I had to go, but I swore to myself that I was not giving up. There had to be a way.

When I mentioned my problem to Aunt Beatrice, she shook her head. "I don't think I ever saw a prune box," she said. "When I'm uptown I'll take a look in the Arthur Avenue Market." She took her pocketbook out of her shopping bag and lowered her voice. "Don't tell your mother," she said, handing me two dollars that smelled of face powder. "Your mother says if I give you things, the other kids will get jealous. Anyhow, I'm not working right now, so I haven't got much to spend on anybody. Hold on to that money in case your friend finds what you're looking for."

"Thanks," I said. "Thanks a lot." I must have sounded kind of awkward or something, because suddenly she broke into her big-bosomed smile. She grabbed my face

41

in her large hand and squeezed it so that my lips were pushed into a pucker, and then she kissed me in her loud Italian way. She seemed like a much older woman, but, actually, she was only about thirty or maybe less.

On Sunday, I waited again for Dino to show up. I remembered how one day I asked him why he didn't hang out on his own block. He said, "The guys over there are jerks. I rather come here and watch stickball." I could tell by the expression on his face that he wasn't going to answer any more questions.

I waited around for about a half an hour and then I saw him turn the corner and I ran to meet him before he disappeared. "Did you find it?" I said.

"Hey, give me a break, kid," he said. "I'm a busy guy. But don't worry, I talked to an old man at the market who says he's got one at home. He'll bring it in this week, maybe Wednesday. Did you get the money?"

"Yeah. It's home. Do you really think he'll have it by Wednesday?" I said.

"Oh yeah, he'll have it for sure, unless he drops dead or something. I tell you what, you keep that money and you'll owe me. When you do me a favor we'll call it even. I'll see you later."

"Where are you going?" I said, following him like a loyal puppy.

"Can you keep a secret?"

"Cross my heart and hope to die," I said.

We walked halfway down the block. He paused, looked both ways, and suddenly ducked into the hallway of a building I had never been in. It felt cool and strange and had an odd smell. "Is this where they fly the pigeons on

42

the roof?" I said.

He smiled in his simian way. "Pretty smart for a little kid." I followed him up the five flights of stairs. "The bird man is a friend of mine," he said, before pushing open the door to the roof. There was no one there. The pigeons were noisy in their large cage. There were white leavings and feathers on the tar-black roof.

I looked into the distance and saw the East River and beyond it the flatlands of Queens. To the south I could see the New York skyline. "There's the Empire State Building," I said.

"Yup! "he said, leading me around to a shed. "How do you like this?"

"What is it?"

"It's a kind of clubhouse. I hide out here sometimes when I don't want to be bothered. Come on in, I'll show you."

He lifted the burlap bag that covered the opening and I followed him in. He searched himself for a match and then lit a candle. There was an old mattress on the floor with brown stains on it and a few comic books.

"I came up here to have a little rest," he said, stretching out on the mattress. "You want to snooze a while?"

"I don't know," I said, intrigued by the adventure but afraid of something about his expression that had changed. "Maybe I better go home. My mother might be looking for me." There was no room to stand up in the shed, so I sat close to the entrance. The sound of the pigeons seemed louder, as though they were agitated. "What if the man comes?"

"Don't worry, he works on Sundays. He works at

43

that movie theater on 116th Street. Come on, lie down for ten minutes and then we'll go back down to the street."

"I better go now," I said.

"If you can't wait ten minutes then maybe you ought to forget about the prune box. I thought you promised me a favor."

"I did."

"Then come over here and lie down. I won't bother you. I'm just your friend. I like you."

I gave in and lay down next to him, leaving some space between us. He took his time and didn't say anything for a while. Then I could feel him move closer to me. My back was turned to him and I tried to pretend that I was asleep. When he pressed himself against me I said, "What are you doing?"

"Nothing," he said, "I just want to rub up against you for a few minutes. It makes me feel good. I guess you don't know about that yet."

"About what?" I said. My knowledge was so fragmentary that it bordered on complete ignorance. Not having arrived physically, I could not imagine what he was talking about. I could feel that he had an erection, and he kept pushing at me. He started to breathe heavy, and his breath was hot at the back of my neck.

"Don't you ever feel good down there?" he said.

"I don't know. I think I better go now."

"Just one more minute," he said. "I'm almost done. You want to take down your pants?"

"No!" I said and pushed away from him.

He grabbed me by the arm. "All right! All right! We'll do it this way."

"What do you want to do?"

44

"Just shut up for a minute you little bastard," he said, and started pushing against me again. His arm slid around my waist. He was sweating and I could smell him. He smelled like dirty clothes.

"Why --"

He stopped me with a grunt and then his grip on me relaxed and he pulled back.

I stood up and said, "I'm going. I don't want that prune box anymore."

He laughed. "You little jerk. There never was any prune box. Now beat it, and if you say anything to anybody I'll beat the shit out you. Do you understand?"

My face was flushed and I ran blindly towards the door to the staircase. I knocked against the pigeon coop and one of the wire lids opened. The birds panicked. I cried out in a cloud of dust and flapping wings and grabbed at something to steady myself. It was a cast-iron pipe. The birds flew up and scattered. I reached the door and leapt down the steps two and three at a time, my sneakers squeaking on the stone, my hand sliding along the banister in the cool dark hall.

6

Meeting the Enemy

The shoe shine box I finally made fell far short of the one I had dreamt about. And the occupation itself involved mostly a lot of walking and a sore shoulder from the leather strap. I had a few customers, but I did not do a very good job of shining their shoes. I got black polish on one man's white socks, and the rags I used did not produce much of a shine. I walked down one avenue and up another, muttering: "Shine, Mister? Shine, Mister?" After a while it sounded like begging: *Please, Mister, let me shine your shoes.* It was embarrassing and a waste of time, so I quit and took up making model airplanes.

There was a candystore at the corner that sold model airplanes. The owner, Mr. Rosen, said that he was thinking of hanging up a few completed models, because it would be good for business. "And," he said, "I'll put a price on it, already, you should make a few bucks."

I paid twenty-five cents for my first kit. There was a picture on the the box of a Curtiss JN-4, a World War I fighter plane nicknamed "Jenny." The picture on the box showed the biplane in action, a pilot in goggles, his scarf blown back, his machine guns blazing. I was almost eleven that summer, old enough to go to the movies on Saturday morning with my friends, some of whom were taller and could pass for twelve or thirteen. I had just seen *The Dawn Patrol*, an English movie about the Royal Flying Corps in France. The planes were still swooping through my mind

46

when I bought the model. At times my imagination was out of control. The Jennys emerged from a cloud bank at dawn, and above them suddenly there were three Fokkers, red as blood against the blue sky. I shoved the stick forward and went into a steep dive that threatened to tear the wings off the Jenny, and then I pulled back and opened up the throttle. The swooping Fokkers were caught off guard as I completed the rising loop that brought me behind them. I opened up with both machine guns, feeling the heat through my gloves, and smelling the fumes of the exploding bullets. Pieces of the tail and fuselage in my cross hairs splintered away and then the whole plane blossomed into an exploding flower and spun out of control, leaving a long trail of smoke before it crashed into a ghostly field, still streaked with morning fog.

For me, building model airplanes was mostly daydreaming. The actual construction was slow and difficult and frustrating. What came out of the box that inspired my dreams was only a flat piece of balsa wood with the parts printed on it and a sheet of instructions that looked to me, at first glance, like a secret message in a movie about the ancient tombs of Egypt.

I was working at a round table in the living room one day when Mr. Campbell, the landlord, arrived unexpectedly. My mother looked startled. She had been scrubbing clothes on the washboard in the kitchen tub. She dried her hands on her apron and gave herself a quick glance in the mirror on the bathroom door. "Who is it?" she said.

Mr. Campbell nearly filled the doorway with his height and heft, but spoke in the polite voice of a gentleman, holding his hat in his hand. "As long as I was here I thought I would stop in to see how you and your

47

children were getting along."

She looked at herself and the basket of laundry on the kitchen table. It was a small room, made smaller by the bathroom, the sink and tub and icebox. "Everything's such a mess," she said. "Come into the living room and I'll put on some tea. You've met my son Robert."

"Oh, yes," he said, reaching out his enormous hand. There was no escape, so I let him have his crushing squeeze without showing any sign of pain. I think he was impressed by my composure. Or else he decided in that split moment that I did not like him. If so, he was right, though I could not have said at the time what it was about him that annoyed me. And where are the others? he said.

"They've gone with a church group to Orchard Beach," my mother said.

He raised his eyebrows. "Ah, isn't that a fine thing to be doing on a lovely summer day. And why didn't you go with them, Robert?"

No one called me Robert. I was Bobby and preferred it that way. My mother answered for me. "He's just gotten a model airplane and was going to work on it today."

Mr. Campbell took off his rimless glasses and cleaned them with the folded handkerchief from his jacket pocket. "That's a very interesting hobby," he said. "I'd like to try it myself sometime, but don't you think you should be outside enjoying the sunshine? You can work on your model when it rains." He dug into his pocket. "Look, Robert, here's a quarter. Why don't you go to the ice cream parlor around the corner and have yourself an ice cream soda or maybe a sundae. I bet your friends are all out on a day like this."

48

"You don't have to do that," my mother said. "Anyhow, it's too much."

Before the discussion went any further, I took the money and was gone. I didn't bother to worry about Mr. Campbell's intentions at the time, but eventually it occurred to me that they might have been a little less than honorable, considering the wife and children he had in Queens. He had shown us a photo once, and, sometime after his current visit, he actually drove us out in his Buick for a visit. So perhaps there was nothing to it, after all. In any case, I will never know for sure what Mr. Campbell got for his quarter.

But I remember exactly how I spent it when it became mine. I did not go to the ice cream parlor. No simple pleasures for me. I walked six blocks up Lexington Avenue to the second-hand bookstore near 118th Street. It had no visible name and I never inquired. It was the only one in our neighborhood, and my friends and I simply referred to it as *the bookstore*.

I liked Lexington Avenue. Even its name had a pleasant sound. It was wide and sunny, unlike Third Avenue, which was in the shadow of the El and always seemed gloomy.

Having learned to read early, I had, by now, advanced a bit beyond the Hardy Boys to novels like Jack London's *The Call of the Wild,* and was overreaching myself by browsing through all the bins and shelves of the dusty shop. No one ever stopped me or asked me to explain why I was there. What a compliment! It was like a church for me, a kind of sanctuary. And there were thousands of books, crudely organized into novels, poetry, biography, history, philosophy and religion. All the rest

49

were called miscellaneous. And in every available inch of space there were heaps of books that threatened to break down the system entirely. And there were old magazines as well, and even comic books. And everywhere the hidden spiders were trying to spin their webs around them, perhaps to feast on the worms that were supposed to infest them.

At this moment in my life, I felt as though I were sitting in a theater and the curtain was slowly opening on an important drama. I had begun reading newspapers. *The New York Daily News* cost only two cents, but I usually waited until I found an abandoned copy, even if it was a day old. I had already started a scrapbook of headlines, and every night I listened to the news on the radio. There was a special excitement in the voices of the commentators.

I must have been in the bookstore for over an hour before the old man who usually sat outside walked past me in a narrow aisle. He smiled. "It's all right, it's all right," he muttered. "Take your time." And I thought he chuckled to himself as he made his way to the bathroom in the back of the store. He smelled like his books -- dusty and dry.

It was another hour before I made my choice. It had come down to a couple of novels: *Lost Horizon* by James Hilton, and *The Keeper of the Bees* by Gene Stratton-Porter. I had heard of the movie version of the first, but knew nothing at all about the second. I handed them to the old man, who was now up front again beside an immense cash register that must have been heavy enough to be safe from thieves. "So where did you get these books?" he said. "From the ten cents box outside?"

"I don't remember," I said.

He smiled. "You're not a very good liar, but you

look like a smart boy. So give me ten cents each already and take the books. I have too many. I'll never sell them in a hundred lifetimes."

I snuck away with my bargain -- down Lexington to 116th Street and then east to Third Avenue and into the shade of the El. A train went by overhead and I thought of how I used to sit by the window on Second Avenue before my father died. When I reached the Paradise Ice Cream Parlor, I went in and bought a vanilla cone for a nickel. The woman behind the counter looked like a nurse in her clean white blouse and cap. I ate the cone slowly in order to convince myself that I had done the right thing with my last five cents, and I kept touching the books, a bit too shy to open them in such a public place.

Back home I found my mother in the kitchen leaning over the washboard as though nothing at all had happened and no time had passed. Without stopping her work she said, "How was the ice cream?"

"Fine," I said, disappearing into the living room to have a closer look at my new books. Her voice followed me. "Ralph was looking for you. He said he put some things in the back yard for the clubhouse."

"Okay!" I said. I opened *The Keeper of the Bees* and read the first two pages. I understood the words, but my mind began to wander.

I went down to the yard to have a look at the things that Ralph had found. There were several pieces of wood of various sizes stacked against the fence. Probably Mr. Croteau's way of helping out. He did things like that without talking about them. He and his son Ralph seemed to have a special understanding. They even looked alike.

I examined the wood and the frame that we had

already nailed together. I found the hammer that we hid in the open end of a caste-iron pipe. Cobwebs had formed there overnight and I wiped my hand on my knickers. The wood looked very useful. We wanted to leave openings for a window and a door, even if we only covered them with burlap bags from the market. We were building the clubhouse in the corner of the yard where two fences met. That would cover two walls. I went inside the unfinished structure and tried to imagine how it would look. I squatted down as if I were sitting at a barrel or milk box with a candle on it. There really wasn't much room in the place, and suddenly I thought about some of my smarter friends, who had said I was an idiot for playing with kids like Ralph and for building stupid little shacks in the back yard. They were always reading and arguing, reading and arguing. "The universe can't be infinite you schmuck. It has to stop somewhere, Weinberg would say. And Lesko would disagree. "Why? Why does it have to stop. You can always add one more number or one more mile. The universe can't be finite. Even where there's nothing there's space."

There were six of us in our group. We all went to P.S. 157 and had just finished the fifth grade. We were misfits, drawn to each other by our intelligence and eccentricities. We argued about everything.

When I came out of the clubhouse there was still no one around. I looked up at the clothes lines and fire escapes and whatever part of the sky was visible from where I stood. In that moment the world seemed to be a small and dingy place. Whenever I felt that way I tried to think of the future. I decided to go back upstairs and start work on my model. I was stopped by the sound of voices on the other side of the fence between our building and the building on

52

113th Street. In another moment two faces emerged. They looked like twin brothers. Both were dark-haired and dark-skinned. They were Puerto Ricans. "What are you doing?" I said.

"Nothing!" said one boy, and the second boy echoed him: "Nothing!"

I felt a sudden chill of fear and momentary confusion. Not because they had done or said anything unusual but because I had heard so much about the Puerto Rican invasion. "They all carry knives," Fusari had said. His family had already moved east of Third Avenue.

The boys looking over the fence spoke to each other in Spanish. To me they spoke English with an accent. "We live here now. In this building," said one of them.

"Yeah," said the other boy. "We move here from 110th Street. You know the Casa Maria?"

"The Catholic place for kids?"

"Yeah, right across the street. My name is Pedro. This is my cousin Miguel."

I hesitated.

Miguel nudged his cousin. "*Vamanos! El no le gustan puertorriquenos.*"

They lingered and I went about my business. I didn't know whether or not I should be talking to them. "Sometimes the less you say the better," was my Uncle Charlie's advice.

"What you doing?" said Pedro.

"Just making a little clubhouse for me and my friends," I said.

"*Mire, Miguel, una casita,*" he said. "Very nice! Can we come and see?"

I shrugged. "If you want."

53

They scrambled over the fence and looked around cautiously. "You can sleep here in the night," said Pedro.

"*Las ratas van a mordarle*," said Miguel. And they both laughed.

"You got cigarettes?" said Pedro.

"No," I said.

"Too bad. You could sit in your *casita* and smoke a cigarette like a real *bandito*."

"Who are your friends?" said Miguel. "Are they Italians? Those guys don't like us. My uncle says we are enemies."

"We don't have any enemies," I said. "We just hang out together. We don't bother anybody and nobody bothers us."

"*Hablas como un maricon*," Pedro said, and his cousin laughed.

I didn't like the way they did that -- talking to each other in Spanish and then laughing. There was ridicule in their laughter, even though they were young and still had remnants of innocence about them. Under different circumstances, without the fear and suspicion, we might have become friends. They reminded me in that moment of alley cats who were curious enough to approach you but ran away as soon as you reached out to touch them. And if you were not careful and quick they could scratch you and draw blood.

Suddenly, we saw the huge figure of Mr. Croteau even before the sound of his footsteps reached us from the alleyway. "What are you kids doing here?" he shouted.

"They live over there," I said.

Mr. Croteau gave me a hard glance. "I don't give a damn where they live. They're in the wrong yard and

54

they're in the wrong neighborhood." The forefinger that he aimed at them was as rigid as a gun. "If I see you little bastards in here again, I'm going to throw you over that fence. Now beat it!"

I could tell from his eyes and from memories of my father that he had been drinking. He turned on me, a poor substitute for the larger audience that he needed. "You know who did this?" he said. "You know who let the spics in around the corner? It was Campbell, that lying sonofabitch! He and his partner own about ten houses in this neighborhood. If the landlords don't keep the spics on the west side of Lexington Avenue, we all might as well pack up and move out."

I just nodded to agree with him. I knew there was no point in trying to suggest that the kids might be friendly. In his mind they were the enemy and that's the way it was going to be.

And that's the way it was. The next day we found the clubhouse torn down and the pieces of wood thrown over the fence into the unpaved yard behind the garage, the one with the big old tree that was gradually being carved to death by nocturnal lovers and kids with hatchets. I stared through the fence for a long time. The modest dream of a little space of our own was now part of the general debris and garbage accumulating in the dark and insulted earth of the yard next door. I remembered a picture in *The Daily News*. The civil war in Spain. Some peasants staring at the rubble that was was their village. For a moment I knew how they felt.

7

The Summer of 1939

I woke up from childhood that summer to find that I was living in an immense world. From the moment I started my scrapbook of headlines I began to feel the widening circles of awareness, like the circles that spread away from a center where a stone is dropped in still water. Something had set in motion my desire to explore the world, and with that desire there came great expectations and a sense of danger.

For the first time I was aware of myself in an objective way, as though I were seeing myself through the eyes of others. The passage from innocence to self-consciousness brought with it a need to know myself. I looked in the mirror in my mother's bedroom and toyed with my reflection. When I raised my right hand, why did that image raise his left hand? I stared him down and he sometimes frightened me, as though he had a separate existence. I took long walks. I stood in Times Square and wondered how I could have been born in America, the most powerful country in the world, and in New York, the most important city in the world, and in Manhattan, in the heart of that city. I felt important and special. The whole thing was mysterious. After all, I might have been born in Kansas or in a small village in the Congo or some crowded city in the Orient -- Peking or Kuala Lumpur. I studied maps. I memorized the capitals of states and countries.

As the circles grew larger I also became more aware

of my family and my friends. They came into focus as real people, and I became curious about their origins and their relationship to me. Sometimes I would stare at my mother until she noticed and then I would look away quickly or ask her a question. "Are we Italian?" I might say. "Where was I born? Where were you born?"

She would always say, "I'm American. I was born in New York, and so were you."

"And your mother and father?"

"My mother was born in Campobasso and my father was from Salerno. My mother was five years old when her parents came. It was the year of the Great Blizzard, 1888. My father was born in 1880, and his family came to America in 1881, so he was only a baby. Your father's people came a little later. They were a good family, but --" She hesitated. I waited but she did not go on. Her thoughts seemed to drift away into the sunlight that came through the white summer curtains.

Many of the people my mother talked about were just names to me, but there were a few relatives we visited now and then, especially an aunt in Brooklyn who was married but childless and had a nice house, large enough to accommodate several unmarried brothers and sisters. Aunt Jenny presided over the place like a strict mother, demanding neatness and order.

The people we saw most often were my mother's sister Constance, whom they called Gussie, and her brother Joseph. There was another brother, Michael, who had disappeared and would not surface again for about twenty-five years. He was a gambler who might have had a problem with the law.

And then, of course, there was our immediate

family: my brother and sister and I. Not exactly "orphans of the storm," but bound together by adversity and dependent on our mother for survival. I often wondered how my mother felt about "the missing father." Did she feel, as the others did, that his death was a blessing that made survival possible? She rarely mentioned him.

Though my brother and sister and I had the usual childhood squabbles, we spent a lot of time together. I enjoyed playing games with my brother because I was two years older and could usually beat him by skill or cheating. Our rivalry undoubtedly went back to the time he was born. He was the baby and needed my mother's attention. I was only two and jealous enough to be an infantile criminal. And my sister was a partner in this effort to punish him for becoming our mother's favorite.

In the summer of 1939 my sister was twelve years old and very tall for her age. Something had happened to her that aroused my curiosity. I could see her emerging figure, her young breasts and slim waist. She seemed suddenly to have secrets, things that she whispered to my mother or to her friend Alice, who was a year older. I occasionally tried to catch a glimpse of my sister without her clothes on, but in that small apartment she was careful to protect her privacy.

I had heard descriptions of the sexual experience, but I still did not understand what it was all about. Even the rough and amusing advances of my sister's friend Alice only put a dent in my innocence. She was a tall girl of thirteen with the body of a woman. In that spring and summer she seemed to grow like Alice in Wonderland, until all the buttons on all her dresses seemed about to pop. She laughed at everything and her sense of morality was as wild as her hair. When no parents were around in our apartment or hers, she would tease me. On one occasion she said, "I'll show you mine if you show me yours. Take off your pants." It didn't bother her that my sister was there. She undid my belt and my short summer pants dropped to the floor. "What are you doing?" I asked. She howled with laughter and pulled down my shorts to reveal a little finger of a penis, a shy, uneducated creature that responded in the usual way to her big-handed caress. She dragged me onto the bed and lifted her dress to show me hers. Her underwear was stretched between her parted knees. My sister was a silent witness to her friend's attempt to seduce me. Alice managed to get me on top of her, but there was too much of her and not enough of me. Finally, she yelled, "He's too small!" She shoved me aside and pulled up her panties. The adventure was over and I stood there feeling and looking like a complete failure.

Before long, however, I was given some mature instructions by my adoring Aunt Beatrice, who had taken on the job of guiding me through the labyrinth of puberty. How such a hefty and homely woman could have discovered such knowledge I don't know, but she had an intelligent and soothing way of explaining things. She pressed me against her huge bosom and told me what an erection was and why. I slept on a day bed in the living room. Her nightly visits at bedtime became a sort of ritual. Mostly we talked. I told her what I did during the day and what I hoped to do the next day and in the more distant future, a subject that had been introduced into our lives by the impending war and the arrival of the World's Fair.

Her fondness led to fondling and I discovered what all the fuss was about. But the ritual had its limitations, since my mother was usually in the kitchen doing the dishes or reading the newspaper.

In this pre-dawn of puberty I was confronted with another strange situation. My mother had a cousin whose Italian father had married a German woman. This cousin, Leo, was tall and handsome and intelligent but with an edge of moral decay about him. My mother qualified every compliment that she paid him. She thought he probably got his intelligence from his German blood. "But," she added, "German women can't be trusted." She admitted that he was quite handsome, but she also insisted that he had tuberculosis. "He wanted to be a lawyer," she once said, "but he wound up as a con man. He's some talker!" This remark made her giggle for some reason I have never understood.

For a while that summer Cousin Leo would stop by fairly regularly. He said he was a door-to-door salesman and that he was selling a product that would extend the life of silk stockings. I watched him as he used our round table with its glass top to measure out a white powder he then put into small brown envelopes that were perhaps two inches by three. As he did this tedious work, he told me about his travels and all the odd jobs he had worked at. He had been to Maine and Miami and even the West Coast. I admired the deftness of his long-fingered hands as he parted the powder with a single-edged razor blade. I offered to help but he said, "Another time maybe."

And then he told me about his two beautiful daughters. "They're about your age, he said. "You ought to meet them sometime. After all, they're your cousins. I think they'll be in show business someday or maybe the movies. I should get them an agent. Their mother is not around, so I really have to keep my eye on them. I don't want them talking to the wrong people and getting into trouble.

The next time he came by I was the only one home, because Uncle Babe had offered to drive everyone to Orchard Beach in his old Ford and I had promised to meet my friends that afternoon at the the pool in Jefferson Park. The cousin we called an uncle had one of his girls with him. She was eleven years old and very beautiful. Her hair was light and her features were delicate. She looked like a miniature adult, complete with curled hair and makeup, including lipstick and rouge and a touch of eye shadow. Her pleated skirt was knee length and below it I could see she was wearing silk stockings and shoes with a slight heel that made her taller than me.

"I'm taking my little lady downtown for a treat," said her father, who was dressed in a suit that was a little too large for his boney frame. "We're going to Radio City Music Hall to see the stage show. I just stopped by to show her off. Isn't she something?"

I nodded politely, but didn't know what to say. It soon became apparent that it would not be necessary to say anything at all. Mary was a talker and I had the uneasy feeling that she had been rehearsed by her father. "I've heard about you," she said. "My father thinks you're very intelligent, but he didn't tell me how cute you were. Do you think I'm cute?" She posed, turning her head and offering me a profile.

"Sure!" I said. "I like your -- your dress."

"How about my stockings?" she said, lifting her skirt high enough for me to see that they were held up by a garter belt. "Aren't they swell? My father gave them to me. He gives me all my clothes and he tells me what to wear when we go out."

"I never get dressed up to go to the movies," I said.

Her father looked at his watch. "We've got plenty of time," he said. We might as well make ourselves comfortable. He leaned over and lowered his voice. "Do you happen to know if there's any wine in the house?"

I looked in the kitchen closet and found the bottle of home-made wine that old Uncle Gino had brought us one Sunday. He sometimes came to eat with us without his wife, who was too fat or sick to leave their apartment. "Can I have some?" said the girl.

Her father poured himself a glass and said, "Here, you can have a sip of mine." Then he stretched out on the day bed and propped himself up on some pillows. I'm just going to have a look at the newspaper and take it easy for a few minutes, and then we'll be on our way. Why don't you two play a game or something. His daughter came over to him and whispered something in his ear. He whispered something back to her that made her smile.

"What kind of a game would you like to play?" I said.

She shrugged. "What have you got?"

"Cards, dominos, checkers, parcheesi."

She hesitated. I glanced at her father, who was lying back and looking at *The Daily News*. His jacket was draped over the back of a chair and he was wearing blue suspenders over his white shirt. He lowered the paper for a moment and said, "Why don't you play post office?"

"I don't know how," I said.

"She'll teach you," he said, passing his long fingers through his dark hair.

62

"It's easy," she said. "We just need some paper and a pencil. First I write you a letter and leave it in the post office, which will be in the bedroom. And then you answer my letter and also send it to the post office, where I will find it and read it."

Beyond her, on the day bed, her father seemed to be falling asleep. The window was open and the gauzy curtains were stirred by a gentle breeze. A quick fly darted from wall to wall before landing on a potted fern. Everything suddenly seemed very strange to me. The sun was shining, my pretty cousin was scribbling a letter to me, her father was asleep on the day bed, the newspaper on his chest.

"All right," said Mary, folding the piece of paper. "I've got to go to the post office now and mail my letter. You wait here." She went into the bedroom, lingered for a moment for a token passage of time, and then came back. "All right," she said. "Now it's your turn. You have to go to the post office and look for your mail. Maybe your sweetheart has written you a letter." She seemed thrilled by the whole fantasy, but I thought it was all very stupid.

I followed her instructions reluctantly, motivated largely by her flirtatious manner. She must have spent a lot of time in the movies, I thought. In the bedroom it was not difficult to find her letter. It was neatly folded and sitting right there on the bed with my name and address written on it in a feminine handwriting. I wondered how and when she had memorized my address. Perhaps she had an address book in the purse she carried. And maybe she also had a bottle of *eau de cologne,* because there certainly was a dab of something flowery on that letter. I was aroused, though I did not know the full meaning of the word.

I opened the letter and tried to make out her careful script. She must have practiced for a long time to write that way, but the language of her letter did not measure up to her penmanship. In fact, there was a shocking contrast that forced me to read the short note over and over again. *How are you? Isn't it a nice day? Would you like to have some fun? I will show you what I have under my skirt if you show me what you have in your pants. You probably won't notice that I have some hair down there, because it's blonde. How about you?*

I sat there on the bed for a long time, wondering how she could write such things to me and how we could do any of those things with her father in the next room. My encounter with my sister's friend Alice was so traumatic that I didn't really want it to happen again. On the other hand, my cousin was very pretty.

Mary burst into my speculations like an irate wife. "What are you doing in here?" she said. Were there echoes of her missing mother in her tone? Was her father training her as a substitute for a wife who was sick or dead? These thoughts came later on, of course. At the time I didn't know what to think.

Before I knew what was happening she had loosened our clothes. All her behavior implied some revised version of the rules of romantic love. The rules were her father's, of course, and as I looked beyond Mary I could see him in the large mirror on the bureau. He was not asleep on the day bed. He was leaning on his right elbow and looking at us through the same mirror. I blushed and tried to fix my clothes, but she whispered, "It's all right. He told me that we could play this game. He doesn't mind. He taught me how to do it. Just hugs and kisses and make-

64

believe."

"Make-believe what?" I said, my mouth suddenly dry with fear.

"You know! she said with gesticulating eyes and shoulders. "What grownups do when they sleep in the same bed without any clothes."

"You do that with your father?" I said.

"No, he just shows me how people do it. He doesn't want me to learn from the boys in our neighborhood."

She was such a little actress that I could not tell when she was lying and when she was telling the truth. With a little bump and grind she was out of her skirt and standing there with her slender arms lifted like a stripper. Her skin was very white and her panties were very pink. "Are you going to take them off?" I said.

"No!" she said. "But you can have a look." She pulled them down a bit and I looked for the hair she had mentioned but I could not see any. She pulled them up again and stood close to me with her lips pursed for a kiss. I obliged her awkwardly. She was not satisfied. She put her arms around me and pulled my body against hers. "You have to rub up against me, dummy," she said.

"Why?"

"To make your little thing bigger."

"But it's already bigger," I said.

"Oh!" she said, wrinkling her brow. "Does it do anything else?"

"Like what?"

"Like -- you know. Does something come out?"

I had heard this before, but it was still not part of my experience. "No," I said, expecting to be scolded.

65

We continued our childish imitation of adults on my mother's bed but eventually lost interest. She ran through her repertoire of desires, demands, and disappointments, and then put on her skirt and combed her hair. She was all actress. I'm not sure that she had any feelings at all. In the mirror she must have seen her voyeur father lying on the day bed. Perhaps combing her hair was a signal to him that the show was over. When we came out of the bedroom he seemed to be sound asleep, his face turned toward the wall.

I never saw her after that, but I heard, years later, that she died young.

8

"The World of Tomorrow"

There were so many important headlines in the summer of 1939 that I filled my original scrapbook and had to buy a new one. Most of them dealt with the approaching war: GERMAN-AMERICAN BUND DENOUNCES JEWS. NAZI RALLY IN MADISON SQUARE GARDEN. CZECHS COLLAPSE. NAZIS ENTER PRAGUE. SPANISH WAR OVER. FRANCO IN MADRID. THREATS OVER DANZIG. BRITAIN-POLAND TREATY. HOLLAND MOBILIZES. CHILDREN EVACUATED FROM PARIS. GERMAN-RUSSIAN NON-AGGRESSION PACT. POLAND INVADED. WAR DECLARED BY BRITAIN AND FRANCE.

Aunt Beatrice financed my ambitious effort to keep an orderly chronicle of an increasingly chaotic world. She also encouraged me to collect stamps. Sometimes on Saturdays we went to a movie on 86th Street and to the Automat, where we browsed past a counter of hot food and a wall of little glass doors, behind which there were other selections, such as sandwiches, salads, and desserts. You put a few coins in a slot and a door opened. It seemed miraculous to me, a preview of our great future. It was, ironically, the theme of the The World's Fair of New York -- "The World of Tomorrow."

I had fallen in love with the future, with progress

and science. Even the war wasn't going to stop me from dreaming about a new world, orderly and clean, a world in which people lived in peace and reached for the stars.

During the summer of 1939 I saw *Things to Come*, a movie that stirred my imagination and my dreams of utopia. One hot day I found myself walking up Third Avenue, full of vague longings. I had just enough money to get into the Stadium, a musty old theater that showed reruns and triple features. Its marquee was in the shadow of the El. My friends and I did not like to go there because it smelled of insecticide, but it started to rain and I went in.

Things to Come was a journey into the future. It began with a prediction of endless wars and went on into an era of wonderful progress and enlightenment. A global government evolved. Its peace-keeping force was called "Wings Over the World." They all wore white uniforms and defeated the remaining warlords by dropping bombs that contained a harmless "peace gas." War became obsolete and everywhere there was harmony and progress. Eventually, however, progress itself became an issue and people were divided.

I left the theater in a fever of excitement and anxiety. The voice of Raymond Massey boomed in my brain: *Wings Over the World!* But I also heard the voice of an opponent of progress, who addressed an angry crowd and denounced the launching of a space ship that would go to the moon or another planet. I wanted desperately for that space ship to be launched and I wanted to be on it, heading out into the vastness of the sky -- out and away from this old sickly world on the brink of war, and from this neighborhood that was dreary in the steady rain.

The opening of the New York World's Fair at this

crucial moment in history helped me to maintain my optimistic view that mankind wanted peace and that tomorrow would be better. My friends and I made our first visit to this marvelous arrangement of exhibits and amusements as soon as school was out that summer, and we returned often. All we needed was a nickel each way for the subway and fifty cents for an entrance pass that allowed us into all the basic buildings. For another quarter we could get a couple of hotdogs and a soda.

We were a benign gang, all of us eleven or twelve years old and about to start junior high school. In those days we felt that nothing could separate us. We didn't even think about it, though we questioned everything and argued loudly enough in the local library about the nature of the universe to get ourselves kicked out at least twice a week.

We were classified in school as "advanced students" and were referred to only by our last names. The habit would last for many years, as though we each had only one name: DeMaria, Lesko, Weinberg, Quintero, Fusari, Nemerich. I was an Italian-American with blonde hair and blue eyes. We usually gathered at my house because my mother was the only parent who could put up with us. Other parents thought we were loud, obnoxious, and peculiar. We did some very odd things.

Weinberg was Jewish, a fat little kid who always had ink stains on his white shirt. He had sour cream skin and full lips, and was always picked last when we chose up sides for any sport, but he had a quick argumentative mind and stored up information as though it were ammunition.

Lesko was the mad genius of the gang. His I.Q. was some awesome figure that actually frightened his teachers. He was also taller than the rest of us and good at sports in spite of his awkwardness. While I was still reading Big/Little Books and Tom Swift novels, he was reading Dostoyevsky and Tolstoy. He was a pale, desperate looking boy, who might have made a plausible character in a Kafka novel. He would periodically retreat to his bed and literally live there among his books and breadcrumbs and filthy sheets. His Czechoslovakian parents had no idea how to deal with him, so they didn't. His father worked in a wire factory and read the *Racing Form*. His fingers were yellow from smoking and he drank vodka. I hardly understood him when he spoke.

Quintero, who was a year or two older than the rest of us, came from Cuba and was held back a bit until he learned enough English. From a very early age his drawings and paintings were impressive. He would eventually create several large murals for the school.

So there we were in the summer of 1939, one foot in childhood and the other reaching for adolescence, aware of the threat of war but unable to appreciate the reality of it. Along with baseball cards we collected war cards, pictures of military struggles in Europe and the Orient. The Spanish Civil War. The Japanese invasion of China. And day by day our toys were turning into true things that might become personally deadly.

When I told my mother that my friends and I were going to the World's Fair, all she said was, "It's kind of far, isn't it? How much does it cost to get in?"

"We can get there on the subway," I said. All I need is a dollar for everything.

She hesitated. I held my breath. A dollar was a lot of money when your entire income was only sixty dollars a

70

month. She looked at me as though she understood how serious my desire was, and then she went into her room and came out with a dollar. "Here," she said, "but be careful and take a sandwich." She put some apple butter between two slices of Silvercup bread and wrapped it in wax paper. She included a banana and an orange and searched the kitchen for a brown paper bag.

I was the only one on this safari who carried his lunch as though I were going to school instead of on a journey into the future, into "The World of Tomorrow." Lesko always seemed to have more money than the rest of us. He said his father played the horses and tipped him when he had a winner, so that he would not tell his mother.

We met at our house (we all said *house*, though we all lived in apartments). My eight-year old brother pleaded with us to let him come along, but my mother was against it, and so were we. At that age there was nothing worse than having a younger brother, unless it was having a younger sister. I suppose we were all trying to grow up and preferred not to associate with little kids.

I loved the long subway ride, because part of it was above ground in sunlight, and I imagined that it was like a real train, the kind that left Grand Central Station or Penn Station for the outside world. New York was, of course, a world in itself. I had never been anywhere, except to a camp in New Jersey, which we could reach by boat. The fact that the world was coming to New York in the form of a great fair seemed perfectly reasonable to me.

The closer we got, the more excited I became. "I want to see the man-made lightning," said Weinberg.

"How can they make lightning indoors?" said Quintero. "It must be a trick."

71

"It's not a trick," said Lesko, his eyes enlarged behind his glasses.

My mind drifted away through moving patterns of light and over the low attached houses of Queens. Then, suddenly, I saw in the distance the Trylon and Perisphere, rising from the flat landscape, an elongated pyramid of gold beside an immense crystal ball -- the signature and symbol of the Fair. In that moment I knew all things would be possible in the future. I did not breathe for six heart beats and then sucked in the air of a new world.

A ramp linked the station with the entrance. The crowd thickened. The sun grew hotter. We caught a glimpse of the parachute jump and the roller coaster beyond the art-deco exhibition halls, the fountains and lagoons, the little car-trains whose horns played a familiar tune. I recognized it as a passage from "The Sidewalks of New York." Everyone knew the words. It was our song, a New Yorker's anthem:

> East Side,West Side,
> All around the town,
> The boys play Ring Around Rosie,
> London Bridges falling down...

We had arrived at the threshold of the future. I was excited. We stood in line to buy our tickets and then attached them to our belts or shirts. I felt good, as if I now belonged there, a citizen of the Fair and the future. Behind us were the ugly tenement houses of East Harlem, the roaches, the smell of dumped garbage in the back yards. Ahead of us was a clean and orderly world.

We sat on a bench to study the map of the exhibits. There were numbers on the map and a list to explain which exhibits they referred to. We argued about which way to go and which places to visit first. Lesko and Weinberg studied the details and I took the banana out of the brown paper bag and ate it, without offering any to the other guys.

Finally, we decided to walk around without a plan and found ourselves in the Firestone building, watching a demonstration of how they made rubber tires, from the tapping of the sap to the finished product. After that we came to an exhibit that introduced us to television. As we walked in, we stood briefly in front of a television camera, before we knew that such a thing existed. We were amazed and amused to see ourselves on a screen. "How do they do that?" said Quintero.

"How are they going to make money out of it?" said Weinberg. We mugged at the camera and laughed at the other people.

"What can it be used for?" I said.

"Don't be stupid," said Lesko. "It's like a radio, only you can see what's happening."

I didn't get it. "But we already have movies," I said, and then went back for another look. Suddenly, it all made sense. Pictures that fly through the air and arrive in your living room. Fantastic! My lust for the future took a great leap forward.

We wandered through exhibits that portrayed their sponsoring countries as industrial wonders or exotic resorts. There were flags everywhere, some of them representing countries that seemed about to slaughter one another, but not here, not at the Fair. And everywhere outside we heard the simple-minded polka, "Roll Out the Barrel." It was played by the mini-trains and refreshment stands, and often seemed to come out of the air itself:

Roll out the barrel,

We'll have a barrel of fun.
Roll out the barrel,
We've got the blues on the run...

Many of the exhibits we saw praised the advancements of science. We were all in love with science, though we were too young to know much about it. It was just the idea of it that we liked. Logic. Clarity. Improvements like the "kitchen of the future," monorails and helicopters, robots and space ships. "I wish they'd blow something up," said Lesko, the budding anarchist. "All they talk about is peace."

It was a clear day and by noon the sun was hot. We felt the heat in our shoes. We stopped for sodas and hotdogs. My lunch was already gone, but I could not resist joining the others.

A little while later, we were able to get into the demonstration of man-made lightning. It took place in a large dome that kept the immense electrical charge contained. The audience was safe outside the partition. We had seats in the dark and listened to an invisible narrator, who explained what lightning was: "Benjamin Franklin demonstrated the nature of lightning in 1752. It is an electrical discharge that takes place in various ways: between two clouds or even two parts of the same cloud, or between a cloud and the earth. It can take the form of a streak or bolt, a bright flash or brilliant ball..."

And then the darkness was broken by the familiar sound of thunder and the crash of lightning. All this inside a dome that was big enough to feel like the outside world. Incredible! We were startled, half blinded. "Ah!" sighed Lesko the anarchist, his face illuminated.

By the time we got to the main attraction, the line

74

was growing shorter. It was called *Futurama*, the General Motors exhibit. "We won't get in," said Weinberg the pessimist.

"We will so," I said, my optimism magnified by my need for order in the universe. "We have to get in. This is why I wanted to come here in the first place."

"You're full of shit!" said Weinberg.

"Don't you want to see what the future looks like?" I said.

"It's all about cars," he said.

"Then why is there such a long line all the time?"

Even as we argued, we walked towards the wide ramp in front of Futurama. The line moved quickly. From the moment we entered the building I could tell that it was going to be something special. We sat in cushioned cubicles with built in speakers, and we looked down, as if from a great height, at a large city and its surrounding suburbs. This was it, at last, I thought. This was the utopia about which I had been dreaming since I saw *The Shape of Things to Come*. The narrator guided us through the years, and gradually things began to change. It was difficult to tell what was moving, the cubicles or the vast model of the modern world below us.

The illusion was perfectly convincing. I felt transported by this ingenious machine into another time and another place. The cities were clustered in a neat landscape. There were high-rise structures, residential areas, parks and recreational facilities. There were bridges and highways with overpasses and underpasses and clover-leaf intersections that made the flow of traffic smooth. And there were new devices that allowed the driver to cruise automatically, even to lie back and rest, because another

75

gadget made collisions impossible. Electronic eyes triggered breaking systems to keep vehicles apart. The cars were perfectly aerodynamic, air-conditioned plastic bubbles, built for maximum comfort and visibility.

I leaned forward against my safety belt and absorbed every word, every structure and bridge, every forest and river. I felt that it was all real, or, at least, that it was true that the world would be this way before very long. There would not be a war. Progress and Science would triumph after all. We would all leave East Harlem and live in Futurama City. No more cockroaches, no more airshafts that smelled of garbage. No more crime, illness, insanity, or injustice.

I remembered a kid from our school who died when he hitched a ride on the back of a trolley and hit his head on one of the iron structures that held up the elevated subway. They said his skull was fractured and his brains spilled out. And I remembered the account of another kid in the neighborhood who went swimming in the East River. He dove in from a piling and never came up. They said that his head went into the thick and filthy mud. And still another died of a strange blood disease that I could not even pronounce. There would be none of these perils. No wars. No wounded veterans, like the blind man I used to help find his way to the store where he filled his beer container. And each time he would tell me he was blind because he worked in Hollywood where the girls were so beautiful that he could not keep his eyes off them. But everybody on the block knew that he had gone blind in the war. And everybody knew that he was queer for boys and tried to lure them to his apartment. I'm not sure he knew which boy I was, but I always refused his offer of money to help

76

him upstairs.

When our journey to Futurama was over and we came out of the strange, windowless structure, it was like coming out of a movie theater while the sun was still shining. We squinted our eyes and stood there for a moment. "That was great," I said.

"It can't happen," said Weinberg.

"You were right," said Lesko. "It's all about cars."

"No!" I said. "It's about a lot more. It's about everything. It's how we're going to live after all our problems are solved."

"Bullshit!" said Weinberg. "It's all highways and cars."

Lesko agreed. "They don't tell us anything about how the world runs or how the problems got solved. It's just advertising for General Motors."

"Maybe there was a revolution," said Quintero

"Yeah," I said. "Maybe there was a revolution."

"What if it was a Communist revolution?" said Lesko.

"What difference does it make?" I said, without knowing anything about Communism.

He laughed. "Then there wouldn't be any General Motors."

In the late afternoon our eyes drifted across the man-made lake, on which boats that looked like swans were being pedalled. We were losing interest in the future and our eyes were drawn longingly to the illuminated amusement park: the enormous ferris wheel, the Cyclone roller coaster, and the Parachute Jump. The people who had gotten off the train so eagerly that morning now walked by slowly, eating ice cream, hotdogs, and cotton candy. It all looked like a dream in the deepening light. I had seen more science than I could digest in one day, and I was tired. "It must be time to go home," I said.

"Not yet!"Lesko said, his eyes fixed on the amusement park in the distance. "Not until I go on the Parachute Jump."

We echoed his announcement as a chorus. "The Parachute Jump?" The closer we got to the Parachute Jump the higher the tower looked. We stood around a while and watched.

"Yes," he said, like a person possessed. "Who wants to go with me?"

"I haven't got any money," said Weinberg.

"I haven't got any either," I said.

Quintero took up the challenge. "If you can do it, I can."

En route we discussed the height of the tower, the danger involved, and the fact that it was all over so quickly. "It's not worth it," said Weinberg. "Seventy-five cents is a lot of money. I'd rather go on the Cyclone. It's a longer ride and a lot cheaper."

"You won't like it," said Lesko. "Both of you would shit in your pants."

"Oh yeah?" said Weinberg.

"Yeah! I'll even give you the money, just to see you turn green."

Weinberg gave me a consulting glance. I was afraid of heights but I didn't like to admit it. When I said nothing, he assumed I was willing. "Okay!" he said. "But give me the money now."

"Why?"

"Because you might get killed on the Parachute Jump."

"Don't worry. Just wait here and we'll all go on the Cyclone. My sister gave me some extra money."

The attendant strapped them in a seat and buckled on the parachute. They were lifted several hundred feet into the air between guiding cables. They grew smaller and smaller. I wondered whether or not they were scared. My stomach began to churn and my neck was stiff from looking up. There was another attendant at the top who checked them out before they were released into a real free fall. Almost everyone screamed when that happened. And then the chute opened and jerked them to a slow descent. That ended the suspense and there were sighs of relief from the spectators as well as the brave customers.

When they rejoined us I could see that Quintero was pale and that Lesko was elated and smiling, as if he had been yanked out of his more somber mood.

It was my turn to prove that I was brave. All four of us sat in the two front seats of the first car of the Cyclone. Lesko was the only one who knew what it was going to be like. He had been on roller coasters at Coney Island and Atlantic City with his older sister.

As we ascended along the narrow track, I could feel myself slipping into a panic. I wanted to get off, but it was too late. I started to tremble and sweat as we reached the first crest. The downhill run might just as well have been a free fall. My stomach seemed to be in my throat somewhere. I couldn't breathe. All around me people were screaming. Then I let go and screamed also. And I closed my eyes. We were jolted around a tight turn and started uphill again. *Oh, no!* I thought. *Not again!* We rose, we fell, we swerved. I had never felt anything like it in my life. I hated it. I gripped the iron bar in front of me so hard that my hands ached. I opened my eyes briefly and looked over my shoulder to see Lesko laughing at me diabolically, as if he had proven something. Perhaps his superiority. At that point I would have confessed to anything, especially cowardice, if only they would let me off that roller coaster. Again we rose. Again we fell. I kept my eyes closed until we came rocking into the platform. I was the first one out, dizzy, disoriented, my guts about to surrender their contents to the laughing hyenas who called themselves my friends.

My fear of heights was confirmed forever, and it was time to go home and reconsider my love affair with the future.

9

The Church Around the Corner

I was baptized a Catholic, because everyone in my family was probably Catholic from at least the eighth century, when the Lombards gave up their paganism. Italian immigrants were not very good at keeping records, and, after a couple of generations, lost touch with the past. I was always told we came from distinguished families in Italy, but in East Harlem we were considered just another welfare case. We may have been Catholics, but there was never any sign of enthusiasm for religion in our family. Maybe some of the great aunts in black fiddled with their rosary beads and asked the Virgin Mary to cure them of arthritis, but no one ever even bothered to get me confirmed, and if my mother occasionally went to the local Catholic church, she did not take us with her. I once overheard her say to a friend that she didn't really believe *in all that stuff.*

So it wasn't very difficult for her to attend the church around the corner, which was called Methodist Episcopal. We all went there because it was the center of many social activities: the Boy Scouts, Sunday School, monthly dinners, dances and picnics for teen-agers, and, above all, a summer camp.

The congregation was, oddly enough, mainly German from nearby Yorkville, but it was being diluted by Italians and Puerto Ricans. Between Black Harlem and East

Harlem there was an invisible wall. When Benjamin Franklin High School opened in the Italian neighborhood, many Blacks and Puerto Ricans were required to attend. There was a three-way conflict that took many lives. Street gangs made life perilous. The worst offenders were probably the Italians, because the school was located in their turf and there were elements of the Mafia in the neighborhood. When the landlords allowed the Puerto Ricans to move East of Lexington Avenue, the Italians held the line at Third Avenue. I remember vividly how, one morning, the police dragged two dead bodies out of the swimming pool in Jefferson Park. Everybody knew that two more people had to die before the score was settled.

Everybody loved the minister of the church, and he deserved to be loved. He was Rev. Albert Wilson, a wealthy man who lived in Westchester County and had devoted much of his life to running this poor church in East Harlem. He never would admit it, but he probably supported the church out of his own pocket. He was a large man of great faith and energy, with a strong voice and a treasury of anecdotes that sometimes moved his congregation to tears. He was also the man who ran the summer camp, without a staff and without rules. In an outdoor kitchen he bellowed hymns and listened to ballgames on a little radio as he stirred the pot over an open fire.

Since one had to be at least eight years old to attend Wilson's Camp, I had been there a couple of times before the summer of 1939. This time I was determined to graduate from the minister's tent to the greater freedom of one of the two other tents, large structures on wooden platforms with half-walls. I deserved to be put in with the bigger boys. After all, I had just come back from a journey to the future via the World's Fair. I was also on the brink of puberty and feeling adventurous.

My friends were contemptuous of the camp and did not want me to go, because none of them would be there. "What are you going to do there anyway?" said Weinberg

"We do anything we want. This year Jim and I are going to find girlfriends. He's twelve. He knows all about it."

"Who's Jim?" said Lesko.

"He lives on 111th Street."

"Oh!" he said, as if 111th Street were in a foreign country instead of just a block away.

"Where are the girls?" said Quintero.

"The camp is in New Jersey at Port Monmouth. There are houses nearby. Cottages on the beach, and a general store. Sometimes there are girls on the next beach or at the store. I saw one naked once, but her mother made her put her bathing suit back on."

"How old was she?"

"Just a little kid," I said. "Her mother slapped her."

We took a boat from the Battery and then a bus from Keansburgh to Port Monmouth. I carried my clothes in a small duffel bag that my mother had made for me. "Your father had one of these when he was in the navy," she said, as she stitched my name into the denim. She rarely referred to him, and spoke now as though she were daydreaming.

We crossed New York Bay and got a good look at

83

the Statue of Liberty and some large ships. Rev. Wilson pointed out the smokestacks of the *Mandalay*, another day-trip steamboat that had sunk in the bay some years earlier. I leaned over the rail of the top deck and watched the parting waters below and the trail of smoke behind us. It was a long way down and a reminder of how I felt about heights, but it was an adventure, and it was magnified by my imagination. I could go to sea. *Captain Blood.* Typhoons. Hurricanes. The sails ripped to shreds, the rudder jammed. The ship on which my father refused to sail. "Heading for China," my mother had said. "His family hired a lawyer to get him an honorable discharge."

The camp was on a poor stretch of beach west of Sandy Hook. A bunker fleet and the factory that turned the catch into fertilizer had ruined the beach. Dead fish washed up and the chimneys made a terrible stench. Most of the boys, however, got used to the beach after a while, in spite of its condition. This year there were a couple of small boats tossed up on the beach by winter storms to add to the devastation and to the games that the boys played. To top things off, the place seemed to be a graveyard for horseshoe crabs.

It was not Atlantic City, but when you came from the hot streets and dirty back yards of East Harlem it didn't look all that bad. There was space and water and even good air, when the wind was right. There was a crude baseball field marked out in the sandy area between the cooking shed and the narrow asphalt road that smelled of melting tar in the hot sun. Along the road there was a row of utility poles that leaned this way or that, depending on how well they withstood the hurricanes or winter storms. One of them served as a foul-line marker for the baseball field. Rev. Wilson had umpired games there since before World War I. He called the balls and strikes with such confidence and authority that no one ever dared to argue with him.

I played ball occasionally, but was still not big enough for the serious encounters between Wilson's Camp and some local softball teams. This was the domain of the oldest boys and some young men who came to the camp to help out, some of whom would soon wind up in military service, including the two sons of Rev. Wilson. The names Goodhart, Schumacher, Pollacek, Fox, and Vandervoort among others lurk in my memory.

If I was too young for baseball, I was even less eligible for the art of seduction. My experience had been limited to a few juvenile encounters, but the recent changes that had been taking place in my body had heightened my interest in girls, though I was still on the boyish side of puberty. I was uncertain about what I was supposed to do or say. *Kissing?* I guess so, though I really didn't see the point. It didn't feel like much. *Looking* was all right. At least you didn't have to apologize. Perhaps I was a natural born voyeur. *Touching?* It was usually taboo, but my sister was teaching me how to dance. I saw it as a way of getting close to a female body. *Intercourse?* I wasn't exactly sure how it was accomplished. I had drawn a naughty picture once that I showed to my friends. They laughed because I depicted the girl with a vertical line on her lower belly. Quintero the artist drew me a more realistic picture. "You've been looking at your sister," said Weinberg. Quintero, the Cuban, flew into a rage, threw a punch at him and called him a *Jew bastard.* Weinberg took off more quickly than we thought possible, considering the

85

excess weight that he carried.

My friend Jim from 111th street was Irish and plastered his unruly hair down with pomade. It made him look like his red-faced drunken father. But he was young and had good features. He, too, had promised to find himself a girlfriend that year. The day after we arrived, we climbed over the rotting jetty and visited the next two beaches, both of which had summer cottages for rent, but all the people we saw seemed old to us. They lounged in wooden chairs and read newspapers or books. One man smoked a large cigar and wore a knotted handkerchief on his head. His wife looked enormous in her skirted blue bathing suit. Her bosom seemed to be sitting on her lap. There were some small children here and there, but no girls of the kind we were looking for.

Back at the country store, Jim bought me a Royal Crown Cola and we sat outside to watch the cars go by on the road. The family that ran the store lived in the rest of the house. A girl appeared. She was wearing a summer dress with a cotton belt that was tied in a bow at the back. She went upstairs for a few minutes and then came down again and paused to look us over. None of us said anything. When she went into the store, I half expected her to disappear forever, but within five minutes she appeared with some egg boxes. This time she said, "We have chickens in the back. Would you like to see them?"

"Sure!" said Jim.

"Sure!" I said, echoing him.

We followed her. I guessed that she was an inch or two taller than me but not much older. There was a chicken coop and a shed behind the house and store. "I have to get some eggs," she said, and showed us how she did this. In fact, she explained everything she did as though we were young or stupid. She kept reaching into the hen house until she filled two boxes with eggs. "How about that!" she said. "Two dozen! Must be the new feed." She put the boxes down on a cedar stump and then dipped her hands into a barrel of water. "It comes from the rain pipe," she said. I bet you come from Wilson's Camp."

"Yeah!" said Jim.

"Yeah!" I said.

"What's your name?" she said, looking directly at me and not at Jim.

"Bobby," I said.

"Jim," he said, though he wasn't asked.

"What's yours?" I said.

"Ida Moon," she said with a broad grin.

"That's a nice name," I said.

"Some people think it's strange."

"I don't."

She continued to ignore Jim, and after a few more minutes he left. "I have to bring these eggs inside," she said, but I'll be right out. "Why don't you wait for me under that shade tree and I'll bring you some lemonade. It's in the icebox in the house and it's real cold."

I sat under the tree and waited obediently. She was a pretty girl with a broad face, a dimple in one cheek, full lips, and a hint of a bosom. She came out with a small blanket and a pitcher full of lemonade. The glasses were originally jelly jars. I caught a glimpse of her mother, who came to the screen door as if to see who I was. She was wearing an apron and must have had customers waiting, since she disappeared almost immediately. I was nervous, but Ida looked perfectly at ease, as if everything she did and said was pure instinct. She told me all about her family, her dog, her best friend, her school, and all the movies she had ever seen. "Do you like the movies?" she said.

"Of course," I said, "but not the mushy ones that make the ladies cry. And I don't like cowboys who sing."

"I like their horses," she said. "I wanted a horse of my own this summer, but my father said I would have to wait until I was thirteen."

I lay back on the blanket with my hands behind my head and thought of *thirteen.* I stared up through the midsummer foliage of the large maple tree. I can still see in my mind the light that filtered through the leaves and the very veins of those leaves, beyond which there floated white clouds in a sea of blue air. "I'm only eleven," she said. "I'll have to wait two more years. But I have a bicycle. Maybe we can go for a ride later."

I was relieved to hear that she was only a few months older than me. "I don't have a bike," I said.

"There might be an old one in the barn," she said. "I'll have a look later."

She poured me more lemonade, and I sat up on the blanket with the distinct feeling that I was sitting at a table and she was playing hostess or imitating her mother, whom she resembled. Perhaps she had felt the need to find a boyfriend that summer, just as I had had the blind impulse to find a girlfriend.

Our limited conversation led, in all innocence, to personal questions. "Where do you live?" she said.

"New York," I said.

"Do you like it there?"

A dozen things entered my mind, but all I managed to say was, "It's all right." I was embarrassed by my

88

shyness. By comparison she seemed bold and mature.

Eventually, she got to the point, as efficiently as she had gathered and arranged those two dozen eggs. "Do you have a girlfriend in New York?" she said.

"No," I said.

She gave me a big-eyed smile. "Maybe I can be your girlfriend."

All of a sudden talking to girls seemed real easy. I was expecting a lot more stumbling and mumbling. "Sure," I said, and we fell into a relaxed conversation about street games and bicycles.

Before long, however, her father appeared at the back door in a khaki shirt and red suspenders. "Hey little girl," he said in a harsh voice, "get in here and help your mother."

She leapt to attention like a soldier, but whispered to me before she left: "Can you come tomorrow about the same time?"

I nodded and did. She was waiting under the maple tree, but there was no blanket, no lemonade. "Was your father mad?" I said.

"He's always mad," she said. "And now he's afraid there's going to be a war. His family came from Germany." Her smile faded. "Maybe next time you should meet me in the lane just before you get to the store. That narrow lane through the high reeds. I'll bring my bike. I can't find the other one, but we can share."

The reeds were alive with sounds: the whispering and rustling, the invisible frogs and cicadas, mosquitoes humming like little vampires. The ground was moist and printed with the large tires of a tractor. "It's a short cut to the beach," she said, "but nobody hardly goes this way." I tried to ride her bike with her on the back fender but I couldn't do it. It was a boy's bike, and she told me to sit on the bar, which was like sitting between her legs. She seemed very strong and had no trouble peddling along the soft path. I was glad no one was around to see us. I had learned from *The Hardy Boys at Mystery Lake* the importance of being heroic.

When she stopped the bike and got off I had no idea what she had in mind. She must have found my innocence annoying, because she became impatient and said, "You can kiss me if you want to."

It was the dreaded *kiss*. I knew it had to come eventually, but I didn't really know how to do it. These things seem to come more swiftly and naturally to girls. "Do you want to?" she said.

I cleared my dry throat. "Well, yeah!" I said, without an ounce of romance. It was her challenge and it was up to me to pass the test. The chorus of insects became louder. The sun became hotter. The bike was between us, leaning on its kick-stand. I advanced, lips first, unable to decide which way I should tilt my head. I leaned on the bike, as if I was about to jump on it and ride away. The rest happened so quickly I can't remember the details. She had come around the bike, or perhaps even leapt over it. Her arms were open. Her blonde hair, parted in the middle, reached almost to her shoulders. "I shouldn't let you do this," she said, and pulled my body to hers. Our lips met and lingered. It felt more like an impasse than a union. I wondered how long we were supposed to maintain this ridiculous position. I could feel my lips pressing against hers and my teeth pressing against the inside of my lips. I was seized by a sudden panic. What if I couldn't

90

breathe? What if I suddenly opened my mouth? I had never even heard of the French kiss, but the possibility at that moment struck me as disgusting. And then the drama ended. She pulled away, as if I had been the offender. "You shouldn't have done that," she said. "If my father knew --"

I waited for her to tell me what her father would do, but she did not go into detail. Would he hit her with his hand? Would he use his belt, as my father sometimes did? And why was she taking the blame, if I was the one who kissed her? "Should we do it again?" I said.

"No, the first kiss is always just one kiss," she said.

She seemed to have access to some secret book of rules. "Why?" I said.

"I don't know why," she said. "That's just the way it is."

"Oh!" I said. "Did I do it right?"

"Sure," she said. "You'll do it better next time. You won't be so scared."

"What about you?" I said. "Were you scared?"

"Of course!" she said, as if I had accused her of being too experienced.

"You mean, you've never been kissed before?"

"Not really," she said, grabbing the handles of the bike and kicking back the stand. And then she looked at the sky as though it were a watch. "Gosh! I've got to go," she said. "I've got to take in the eggs. And remember, this is our secret. Don't you dare tell anybody."

I lingered over a technical point. "Does this mean you're my girlfriend now?"

"Of course, it does. Now get on the bike."

10
Blitzkrieg

On September 1, 1939, the Germans invaded Poland. On September 3, Britain and France declared war on Germany. The headlines were enormous. Our small living room was littered with newpapers that had not been clipped yet, as well as unfinished model airplanes. I was building a German Messerschmitt and a Stuka dive-bomber, both of which I eventully sold to the Jewish man who ran the candy store at the corner. He did not seem aware of the Nazi menace. He simply hung the planes in his window to show that the balsa-wood models that he sold could actually be built. I have no idea how many hours it took me to make them, but all he paid for them was two dollars each.

The Germans moved so swiftly through Europe that a new word was coined to describe their style: *Blitzkrieg*, "lightning war." In the air and on the ground they seemed invincible. Poland was crushed. Norway and Denmark were overwhelmed. Belgium and Holland surrendered. The headlines broke like waves in a storm.

It would be two more years before America got into the war. We were officially neutral, though our bias was clear, except in the New York German community in Yorkville, where many of the members of our church congregation lived. It was an awkward situation for some of them because they secretly approved of Hitler. Others openly opposed him. The controversy came up at the annual church fair, which was held in the church basement and included various games, most of them made by Boy Scout Troop 546, whose leader was Harry Fox. We were a rough and ragged bunch, most of us without uniforms. For the fair I made a swinging pendulum of wood on which I tacked a picture of Adolf Hitler. The object was to throw darts at the picture and win a prize. Three darts for a nickel. A blanket on a rope caught the darts that missed.

The first night of the fair many people played the game, but it was soon apparent that others objected. I arrived the second night to find that the game had been removed. I was very upset, but the scout master explained that we were technically not at war with Germany and that there were many members of the church who thought the game was too political. I was outraged and proud. My first political confrontation! I felt important and grown up. It became a major controversy at the church. Some people even apologized to me.

Between summers Ida Moon and I wrote to each other regularly. Our penny post cards and three-cent letters were juvenile exercises in courtship. We asked each other what we got for Christmas and how we were doing in school and then signed off with love. We made innocent vows that we were destined not to keep.

By the sumer of 1940 Ida had become a formidable swimmer. She had broad shoulders and bumps in her bathing suit that had to be breasts. She was not yet thirteen and I was six months younger. She was a budding young breeder, a country girl who seemed popular with the country boys at the local pool in Port Monmouth. She taught me some games, one of which was kissing under water. I liked the game but she had obviously been playing it with other boys. I felt the first arrows of jealousy. On an evening walk in the asphalt-scented dusk, she assured me that she loved only me. I couldn't tell whether she was telling the truth or had already discovered the convenience of lying. In any case, I was daunted by the speed at which she was rushing towards maturity.

Since Wilson's boys were allowed to roam freely during their two weeks at Cedar Beach, we all became adventurers. We explored the debris on the beach. We followed several narrow roads that went through reeds and farmland, but we often turned back because of the mosquitoes and green flies and the hot sun, or because our stomachs told us that it was almost supper time. There were rumors of a boardwalk in Keansburg, about five miles away. The older boys talked about it. There was cotton candy and a carousel, even beer and girls. I mentioned the place to Ida and she made a face. "My parents say it used to be a nice place but nobody goes there anymore after the big hurricane two years ago. For a special treat we go over to Asbury Park, which has a wide sandy beach on the ocean and a big amusement park with a giant ferris wheel. It's real neat. I'll ask my father if you can come along the next time we go. He already knows about you and me, so I bet he won't mind."

I wasn't sure what she meant by that. What exactly could she have told him? I had met her parents a couple of times and I saw them often in their store, but we hadn't said much to each other. Her mother mostly looked me up and down as though she were afraid I was a juvenile delinquent from the city, and her father asked me if I wanted to earn two dollars for painting the chicken coop.

Since we didn't raise chickens in the city I had no idea how filthy they could be.

The following Saturday we went to Asbury Park in her father's big Dodge sedan. There were six of us: Ida's parents, her kid brother, her aunt and the two of us. It was a brilliant summer afternoon, and the boardwalk was wide and full of people. I was astounded by the size of the waves that rumbled in, shedding white foam in the brisk wind. It was not the first time I had seen the ocean. We all used to go to Coney Island from time to time. Perhaps I had forgotten the days when the surf looked like a series of moving mountains and I ran away from them into the arms of my mother, who looked very odd to me in her bathing suit. I was actually shy of the surf. My mother told me all about how one day I was knocked down by a huge wave. I was only three years old and she was sure that this incident accounted for my hesitance about swimming.

Ida did not suffer from any fear of the sea. As soon as she saw the beach, she was ready to plunge in. And off she went, leaving me trailing behind, a bit embarrassed. When I reached the wet sand where the breaking waves slid up to make a rim of foam, she was already emerging from the sea like some kind of ancient goddess. "Come on in!" she shouted, pushing back her Aryan hair. Her wet bathing suit made her breasts more obvious. They served as a sufficient distraction, and I allowed her to drag me into the water. It was cold, but I pretended that I enjoyed it and broke loose to run through the foam and dive into a wave. Unfortunately, the wave was retreating instead of advancing and I landed in very shallow water. I scraped my belly on the sand, and she laughed hilariously.

I was relieved when she decided to quit being a

mermaid in order to take up some land sports, such as riding in the Whip and on the Ferris Wheel. Her father bought some tickets that looked exactly like movie tickets. They came off a large roll in a booth where a middle-aged blonde with too much make-up played cashier. We started modestly with the carousel, which was, secretly, my favorite ride. Ida shrieked when she caught the brass ring, and then ran to the booth to cash it in for more tickets.

Eventually, we wound up on the enormous Ferris wheel. There was no roller coaster, for which I thanked the God I did not believe in. The cages creaked and the girder-work clock moved sluggishly. From time to time it stopped and we dangled there in the hush and thinness of space with a spectacular view of the sea and sky. "Why do we keep stopping?" I asked.

"Because people keep getting on," Ida said. "We only go around once, unless the man who runs the wheel decides to give us an extra ride. Sometimes he stops a cage at the very top."

"Why?" I asked naively.

"You'll see," she said, cuddling her secret wisdom.

I didn't get the point until it was our cage that stopped. "He's going to wait until you kiss me," she said. "Look down. They're all looking up at us. Do you see them? There's my brother and Aunt Gladys, and my parents, and Freddie Stern with Matilda, who thinks she's such hot stuff."

When I looked down I saw only a mass of upturned faces and the full length of the boardwalk with all its refreshment stands and rides.

"Come on, do it," she said, "before they start whistling and making fun of us. Just do it."

96

I could feel myself blushing. It was an odd kind of stage and I had stage fright, which combined with my fear of heights to paralyze me momentarily."

"Hurry up!" she said and then threw her arms around my neck and pulled my face towards hers. I kissed her mouth, sort of. I could feel my nose touching hers. And then I heard the whistles and applause and laughter. My secret was out. Surely, I would be stoned to death by the crowd when we got back to Earth. That little kiss was a confession of early lechery. Now they all knew about my erection and what I did under the blankets at night.

I was tempted to open my safety belt and leap into the gawking crowd, but it would have been a wasted theatrical gesture, since nobody said a word when we finally arrived from our trip on the giant clock. They were either being polite or indifferent. Even Ida's parents gave me a benign smile. "Did you have a nice trip, Sonny?" said her father. I hated him for calling me *Sonny*, but I am sure he meant no harm. Lots of men called us kids Sonny or Skipper or Buddy.

The war news reached us through Mr. Moon's general store. He put a radio outside on hot evenings so that his local friends could gather there on the porch and listen to Gabriel Heater or Edward R. Murrow. One evening I went over from the camp after dinner to see if Ida was around. I found her sitting on the soda cooler, her legs dangling, her eyes fixed on the men, who were drinking beer and smoking. They were mostly farmers, and their pickup trucks were parked nearby. Ida moved over so that I could sit next to her. Then her mother called to her from inside the house. Ida did not seem to hear her. She called again and then appeared at the screen door, towel in hand. "Ida, what are you doing out here with all these dirty men? Come on inside. I have some fresh lemonade for you and your friend."

"Bobby wants to hear the news," she said. "We'll just be a few minutes." Her mother shook her head disapprovingly and went back inside.

I was fascinated by this scene, since I did not have a father and was now beginning to struggle with the problem of approaching manhood. After all, I was about twelve years old and starting to feel taller and stronger, even as I continued to feel awkward and vulnerable. Since I had been keeping a scrapbook of headlines for a year or so and studying maps, the world seemed like a familiar place. "London is a city on fire," reported Edward R. Murrow. "The Luftwaffe is bombing the docks along the Thames and the area around St. Paul's Cathedral, which stands proud and indomitable in the midst of ruins and flames." Murrow's voice was very dramatic and the whole scene came alive in my mind.

Afterwards, the hushed gathering listened to an even more dramatic commentator, the real spellbinder, Gabriel Heater. "There's good news tonight, my friends! A small band of valiant airmen in six RAF Spitfires held twenty-four bombers at bay over the Channel after downing eight planes in the fighter escort. The Messerschmitts were no match for the new Spitfires. President Roosevelt has expressed his sympathy once again for those who are suffering through the Battle of Britain, but once again he has assured his fellow Americans that he will not involve American troops in the European war."

"Damn right!" said one of the farmers. After the brief report came some grumbling, which developed into an argument over whether or not we should "get into it."

The light was beginning to fade. Ida's mother appeared again and spoke more firmly. "You get in here. Now, young lady. And tell that boy to get back to his camp."

Before Ida went in she said, "If you want to see a haunted house, meet me here tomorrow, early." She was gone before I could say anything, and I went off with visions whirling in my agitated mind.

The next day I came to the store and bought a soda. Mr. Moon grunted something that sounded like "G'mornin." The man next to me, who smelled of sweat, asked for a pack of Wings cigarettes. "I guess you heard about Charlie Johnson," he said.

"Yup!" said Mr. Moon. "They say he was driving drunk."

I went outside and looked around but I could not see Ida anywhere, so I started walking down the road towards the path that cut through the reeds. Pretty soon she showed up, running and calling out. When she caught up to me she said, "I had to do the eggs." We both laughed and then she took me by the hand and led me down to the beach. We were careful to avoid the dead horseshoe crabs. The tide was out and the smell was unusually strong. "The house is really haunted," she said. "I'm not kidding. It's just past the second jetty. It was a summer place with a bar and rooms upstairs. They say a man was killed there and that his ghost is still waiting for the killer to return so that he can get revenge."

99

"I don't really believe in ghosts," I said.

"Well, that won't stop him from getting revenge," she said. "I suppose you don't believe in God either."

"I haven't made up my mind yet, but I go to church," I said, without mentioning the Boy Scouts.

"I don't like to think about things too much," she said. "Because if you do, you're liable to wind up doing nothing. Anyhow, I believe in ghosts, because where's a person going to go after they're dead? Since they have a spirit, I mean, and can't get into heaven right away."

In my mind I could hear the loud voices of my friends arguing in the library about matters of life and death until we were all kicked out and sat on the steps for a while just cursing at everybody and each other.

Ida stopped and pointed to an old house almost completely hidden in the wild growth around it. "There it is," she said in a hushed voice.

I saw the crumbling brick chimneys and the dark moss on the roof. With its boarded up windows it looked like a blind man lost in a jungle of briars and weeds. We approached cautiously and she showed me some loose pickets in a fence that allowed us to get by the rusted barbed wire. "Have you ever been inside?" I whispered.

"No!" she said. "But I've heard stories."

I was a great believer in logic and common sense. I told myself there were no such things as ghosts, but at that moment my beliefs were shaken and I was ready to forget the whole adventure.

"Are you afraid?" she said, leaning so close to me that I could feel the hard apples of her breasts.

I swallowed twice and said, "No, of course not."

"Good!" she said. "Let's see if we can get in."

There was something exciting in that moment. Years later I thought of it as Adam and Eve all over again. The woman provides the temptation and the man is seduced into sin. Forbidden fruit!

Without tools we could not hope to remove the heavy boards that covered the windows. "It's no use," I said. "Let's get out of here before someone sees us."

"You're not afraid, are you?" she said. "You don't even believe in ghosts. How can you be afraid?"

"I'm afraid of the living not the dead."

"You're not supposed to be afraid of anything," she said. "You're a boy. A man! If anything happens, I expect you to save me." A hint of a smile betrayed her. I tried not to think about running away with her on my back. She was bigger than me and probably heavier.

It was Ida who found a way in -- a broken pane of glass in a narrow back door. We pushed aside cobwebs and spiders scampered into the rusty shadows. We broke another pane of glass for more light. In a few moments we could see that we were in a barroom. "Gosh." she said, "It's really creepy. It looks as though nothing here has been disturbed for years. Look at the drinks on the bar. And the way that big old clock has stopped. And look at that there calendar. July 3, 1922. Almost twenty years ago. Summertime. That must be the day the man was shot dead."

"How do you know all this?" I said.

"I heard my father and his friends talking about it one day."

"So, how come other people haven't come here?"

My question seemed to be answered from another part of the house with a loud thump. I could feel the hair stand up at the back of my neck, and my mouth went dry. We were frozen there for a long moment, and then, like a crack of thunder, a door was smashed open and someone or something was standing there with a bloody axe. "What the hell do you think you're doing?" the creature roared and flung the axe in our direction.

In blind terror we dashed for the door, both of us screaming like girls who were about to be hacked to pieces. We didn't stop running until we were back on the main road in the hot sun, inhaling the fragrance of hot asphalt. I stopped on the road to let Ida catch up to me. We were both damp with sweat and breathing heavy. "Boy!" she said. "You sure can run fast."

"Yeah," I said. "I run in the park and along the river."

Her face was flushed, her eyes wild with wisdom. "Now, do you believe in ghosts?"

"Sure!" I said, not only to please her, but because it was almost true.

11

Coming of Age

With puberty and hormone upheavals there came revelations and problems. I started to grow rapidly without realizing it at first. One day Aunt Bea gave me a letter to mail. I went down to the mailbox, which was bolted to the lamppost at the corner of Lexington Avenue and 112th Street. There was a time when I had to climb up to the box to put the letter in. Suddenly, I found myself staring directly at it. I rushed back home to report to Aunt Bea that somebody had lowered all the mailboxes. She laughed and her belly and bosom shook like jello. When she explained, I went into my mother's room to look in the mirror. "Is that me?" I asked some invisible witness.

I was getting taller, but I would never catch up with the two tallest members of our gang, both of whom were a year older and would soon be six feet tall. On the other hand, I was rapidly improving as an athlete, and on the playground track in Jefferson Park I was soon outrunning everybody. Discovering what my body could do was a series of thrilling experiences that went beyond my muscular legs. I exercised on the parallel bars and other cold metal outdoor equipment. Sometimes we competed lifting rocks and logs where the FDR Drive was still under construction. We threw bricks into the river to see who could throw the furthest. We played hardball and softball and football and basketball. Once I suggested that we build a raft to cross the East River, but nothing came of that idea except a few arguments about the wild and dangerous currents in the river, and some jokes about turds and scumbags (condoms) from the raw sewage.

I looked more often in the mirror, not only at my face and arms and legs, but at my more private parts. What looked to me like a shy peanut the year before was beginning to emerge as a real penis. And it had the peculiar habit of growing hard. It didn't take me long to figure out what to do about *that*.

My mother tried to tell me about adolescence, and about the Jewish boys who celebrated their *bar mitzvah* at the age of thirteen, but my friends and I knew all that stuff. We spent most of our young lives in the street or the park or the library. We looked up dirty words in the unabridged dictionary and we searched for books that contained photographs of naked women. Lesko, the real reader of the gang, read us passages from the novels of James T. Farrell and D.H. Lawrence. He was a confessed atheist and made jokes about the Catholic Church.

Salvator Fusari blushed and said, "Our priest told us that if we jerk off we might go blind."

"Do you believe him?" said Lesko.

"I don't know," said Fusari, "but my mother took me to the eye doctor and he said that I need glasses." His cheeks blossomed into pink as he smiled.

Weinberg had nothing to say for a change, because, in spite of his *bar mitzvah* he had not yet reached puberty. I, on the other hand, was a two-year veteran, and enjoyed teasing him.

The only thing I did without the gang was to join

the Boy Scouts. They made fun of me for that. The Boy Scout troop met in the basement of the Methodist Episcopal Church on 111th Street, just around the corner from where we lived. It was my sister who first belonged to the church gang, but eventually I was also drawn in. None of my friends went to church, except maybe Weinberg, who went to Hebrew School and probably to synagogue services of some mysterious sort. I rather liked our church. It was made of red brick and had a tall steeple and a belfry. There were cushions on the long, curved pews, and there was a choir loft where the pipes of the organ rose into the Gothic tower, and another kind of organ was destined to impregnate my sister's friend Alice (she of the apple-hard breasts). There were also stained glass windows like the ones in the Catholic Church a few blocks away in the more Italian part of East Harlem.

Arthur Vandervoort was our scoutmaster and the organizer of Troop 546. He was the sort of man that every boy dreamed of having as a father. He seemed to know everything. He was kind but strong, which he had to be in that rundown neighborhood. Organizing a troop was not an easy task when half the kids were from very poor families that knew a thing or two about violence, about drunken fathers and drug dealers and street gangs. For street-smart kids the Boy Scout motto, "Be Prepared" had some unique meanings. Most of us could not even afford a uniform. We would come to the meetings with only a scarf or maybe a scout shirt. Only two or three boys had the whole outfit, and my envy and desire was so intense that at times it felt like physical pain.

After Pearl Harbor, Mr. Vandervoort went off to war and John Goodhart took his place. Later on, he too

105

enlisted and the troop was taken over by Harry Fox. When he left, the troop deteriorated into a Friday night roughhouse recreation group. But before that happened we had a great triumph at a big Boy Scout jamboree, held in an enormous armory somewhere in Manhattan.

There were troops from all over the city, most of them fully dressed and well equipped. The armory was a huge structure with a wooden floor and grandstands. It was used for military gatherings and a variety of other activities, such as track meets and political rallies. Each troop was given a small area in which to set up. There were markers on the floor and aisles made by posts and flags. I kept looking up at the girders and lights and flags. My mouth was open with awe, and for a moment I could hear my aunt saying in her rough way: "*What are you trying to do, catch flies?*"

The jamboree was a competition among the troops of New York. There were specific events, such as fire-starting, signal-sending, and knot-tying. There were judges. And there was music, noise and confusion, over which a loudspeaker presided. "The next event," said a gigantic voice, "will be the tying of knots."

That was my event. I was armed with nine pieces of rope, each about four-feet long. For a uniform I had only a scarf and shirt. No badges or adornments. Some of the other scouts walked around with medals and whole collections of merit badges on a bandoleer, earned in the comfortable meeting rooms of mid-town Manhattan, and at fancy camps in the country. Our East Harlem gang stood out as a group of ragged poor cousins, but larger and tougher than most of the other scouts. We spoke the language of the street, with its indecent and unscoutlike vocabulary. An official came over to question our scoutmaster about our ages to make sure that we qualified. "Oh, yes," said our leader, "we're a new troop. Some of the boys are late starters." The official walked away with his clipboard and a frown. "Motherfucker," muttered Leon, our pyromaniac. "Fastest flint in the East!" he boasted, and would soon have a medal to prove it.

The God-like voice from the steel girders ordered us to lay out our nine ropes and get set for the knot-tying. I had been practicing for weeks and was very swift. I had also absorbed the secret tips of the Goodhart boys. The bell sounded and I was off the mark like a runner, my adrenaline flowing, my heart pounding. Mr. Vandervoort had his stopwatch in his hand. *Square knot, half hitch, bowline* -- and so on. Nine knots in 29 seconds. I started to undo the knots. Mr. Vandervoort yelled something at me, but I didn't understand. Then he leapt forward, grabbed me roughly by the wrist and pulled my hand upward. "You have to signal the judge that you're finished." One of the judges came over. "What's going on?" he said.

"He finished the nine knots," said Mr. Vandervoort, "and then undid them."

"Too bad," said the man with the clipboard, squinting with suspicion. "You'll have to start again."

I kneeled instantly and whipped through all nine knots again while he watched. "Incredible!" he said. He looked around, but not a hand was raised for another five seconds. I was more than twice as fast as any of them.

Troop 546 was the over-all winner at that jamboree, stunning everybody, including themselves. I treasured my medal. To me it was better than any *bar mitzvah*. It was also the triumph of the tough underdog over the soft upper

107

classes. There was no merit badge for that on the bandoleers of the eagle scouts.

In the fall, I entered Galvani Junior High School, which was just three blocks from where I lived. Never was there a more unpleasant testing ground for male adolescents. There were no girls. The neighborhood was deteriorating and gang conflicts were increasing. The battles among the Italians, Blacks and Puerto Ricans began to involve younger and younger boys. Illiteracy and failures kept some students in junior high until they were seventeen or eighteen years old. Poverty gave rise to crime. Cigarettes and drugs were sold in a candy store across the street from the main entrance to the school, which was an ugly piece of Civil War architecture that desperately needed renovation. A truly Dickensian place with soot marks on the red bricks and courtyards more suitable for a prison. Teachers were openly assaulted in the classroom, and a twelve-year-old entering student was bound to be intimidated by the overgrown underachievers. After a female teacher was raped, a security guard was added to the staff. Many of the teachers were staying on just in order to reach retirement age. They hated working there, but it was too late to find anything better, especially since the depression was not over yet. A lot of them were well educated Jews, who were once proud of the schools they worked in. The main business of the faculty at P.S. 83 was to prevent crimes, though occasionally a few students came along who showed an interest in education. That was us, and we were not too popular with the bad guys.

Fortunately, there was the Boys Club of New York, just a block away. Everyone seemed to respect it, perhaps because it provided recreation and not education. It was a large six-story building with a swimming pool, a gym and meeting rooms for special clubs. No bathing suits were allowed in the pool, and there was a lot of horsing around. The favorite game was snapping a towel at another boy's genitals or rear end. The boys were divided into two groups: below the age of twelve, and twelve to sixteen. They swam at different times, on the assumption, I suppose, that the young kids were innocent and the older ones were nasty. When I first qualified for the older group I was stunned by the largeness of their sexual equipment. Later on I was simply impressed, but I was never completely comfortable with the arrangement. I was afraid I might get a sudden erection and sometimes did, in which case I had to stay in the water until things calmed down.

Among the special activities was a stamp club. I had started collecting stamps about the same time that I started my scrapbook of headlines. I saw an ad in a comic book that promised a mixture of two hundred foreign stamps for one dollar. I showed the ad to Aunt Bea and she gave me the dollar. "That's a good hobby for a boy," she said with her immortal smile. By the time I decided to join the stamp club, I had a collection crudely mounted in an album. None of it was valuable, but the direction of world affairs made me more and more interested in it.

The man who ran the club was Robert J. Alexander, a graduate student at Columbia University, whose father was on the faculty. Mr. Alexander, as I called him in those days, was a political idealist of the left, who devoted his time freely to the boys. When I made my first inquiry in the Boys Club office, I was told that all I had to do was to show up on Tuesdays at 4:00 PM when the stamp club met in room 302. I was shy and nervous, never having done this sort of thing on my own before. I had just turned twelve.

The game room in the lobby of the building was always busy in the after-school hours. Ping-pong and knock-hockey contributed their share of noise, but most of it was the sound of growing boys running around in long pants or knickers, adolescents in perpetual motion. Shirts and ties were still required in the local schools, especially in the Catholic school nearby, but now the ties were slipped open and the sleeves were rolled up.

I found the staircase and made my way up to the third floor. Suddenly, everything was quiet and there was a long hallway with numbered doors. I found 302 and stood before it listening and uncertain. There were voices. I was tempted to give it up and made excuses to myself: "They were probably older guys with real collections, and it was probably too late to join anyway." But I tapped gently on the door and waited. Nothing happened. I knocked again. This time the door opened and I was confronted by the terrifying idiot face of a boy with broken teeth, who shouted at me: "What the fuck do you want? Beat it! We got a meeting in here." He slammed the door in my face. I walked away, stunned and confused. A few seconds later, I heard someone behind me. I expected it to be the same crazy guy, but it was a man with a gentle, reassuring voice. "Wait," he said. "Don't be afraid. That boy is a trouble-maker but he's harmless. Come on back. There's plenty of room for you."

This was my first meeting with Mr. Alexander, a young professorial man with glasses and an unathletic body. It proved to be the most fortunate thing that ever happened to me. In another minute I might have been down the stairs and gone.

One Saturday he took the members of the stamp club to his house for lunch. He lived in Leonia, New Jersey with his parents, across the Hudson River, beyond the George Washington Bridge. I thought of the World's Fair and of the GM exhibit called "Futurama." He lived in a real *house*. Everybody else I knew lived in an apartment, except maybe Ida Moon, who lived over the family store in Port Monmouth. We met Mr. Alexander's father, a tall man who looked just like a college professor in the movies. He smoked a pipe and petted a dog named Dostoevsky ("Dusty" for short). The rest of the house, including his mother, seemed to be a set for some wonderful movie about well educated, comfortable Americans. It was all so clean and orderly and civilized. The reality of this way of life was my latest revelation, and as soon as I experienced it, I made it my goal in life to escape from East Harlem and to live in a house in Leonia. I repeated the name of the town several times in my mind and then said to Mr. Alexander, "That's a pretty name for a town.

"Is it ?" he said to me, as though he had never given it much thought. And then, in another moment, he seemed to understand. "Yes, yes," he said, "a very nice name." Later on I decided that to him it was all very ordinary, all very typically American, and that possibly his interest in the poor neighborhoods of New York was a bit like slumming. But deep down I knew this was not true. He was the most honest man I ever met and his compassion for the masses was genuine. To him the new war was a personal agony, and he was willing to fight to rid the world of dictators like Hitler and Mussolini.

111

Eventually, he joined the Army Airforce, but refused to be a commissioned officer.

Before all that happened, I was invited often to his house and to outings in the city, including dinner at a real restaurant downtown, the *Champlain*, after which we went to a real play at a real theater. The play was a revival of *Winterset* by Maxwell Anderson, starring Burgess Meredith, who also starred in the movie version in 1936.

The Champlain was in the 'fifties somewhere, several steps down from the sidewalk. It was like descending into Paris. There were posters on the walls-- the Eifel Tower, Chartres, the Arc de Triumph. I absorbed everything in the dim light. It was all new and exciting. "I thought you might like this place since you are now studying French," said Mr. Alexander.

I did not tell him how much I hated French and how difficult I found it to speak or read or understand. I just smiled and pretended to read the menu that the waiter had handed me.

"What are you going to have?" he said.

I couldn't even pronounce most of the items. and I was too embarrassed to ask what anything meant. He, in turn, seemed determined to let me find my way through this maze of French dishes. I played the game and chose something simple. "*Lapin,*" I said, without knowing what I was talking about.

He raised his eyebrows. "And why not?" he said. "But I think I will have the *coq au vin.*"

I didn't much like the sound of that. I didn't think even the French ate that part of any animal. I caved in at last and asked him what it was. When he told me, I was relieved. "Sounds good!" I said.

"I'm sure the *lapin* is good too, but --" he hesitated. "Are you sure you know what it is?"

I was trapped. All I could do was shrug my shoulders and look helpless.

"It's rabbit!" he said. "Rabbit stew."

"Oh," I said, "I guess I had it mixed up with something else." I had flunked sophistication 101 and he was trying to help me out.

"I think you might be happier with something else," he said. "The *coq au vin* is very good here. I recommend it, especially if you've never had it before."

I discovered that climbing out of East Harlem was not going to be as easy as going to the movies. I had a lot to learn about the most obvious things. Like how to use a napkin in a restaurant. Mine kept falling on the floor, no matter where I put it.

Though I had seen movies that were originally stage plays I had never actually been to a theater. I had walked by them with my friends a hundred times, because walking was free and exploring New York gave us something to do.

The Cosmo, our local movie house, was a harsh and noisy place that sometimes smelled of urine and popcorn, and revealed reality in black and white. Color films were rare events. This theater we went to was a warm and welcoming place, with people who showed us to our seats and gave us programs. The large heavy curtain, the gilded wood, the soft music, the deep rugs all contributed to the soothing atmosphere. It was almost like going to church. And then came the greatest revelation of all -- real people on a large stage with a three-dimensional set. The hush of the audience, the rich, clear voices of the actors. The makeup, the lights, the music from the orchestra pit, and finally the applause, the *bravos,* and the many curtain calls. It was true magic, not just flat, gigantic images on a screen.

On the way home, Mr. Alexander told me all about the Sacco and Vanzetti case, on which, supposedly, Maxwell Anderson's play was based. They were Italian immigrants who were accused of a payroll robbery, in which a guard was killed. I was too tired to understand everything that he told me, and I didn't know what an anarchist was, but I could feel his sense of injustice, his bitterness over the executions of these two men. He had to take off his glasses and wipe them because his eyes had grown misty.

12

Growing Pains

Christmas was always a difficult time for me. I never had enough money to buy gifts for anyone, and I never expected much. It was easy to get bitter. There were times when we could not even afford a Christmas tree. We always went looking on Christms Eve, because, at the last minute, the dealers would sometimes throw the trees away, or just abandon them as they leaned against a brick wall with torn movie posters. One such mutilation produced "The ...rapes of Wrath." My friends thought it was hilarious, but I didn't. I yearned for a good Christmas, something out of the movies. As a compromise I tried to dream within reason -- a few stamps, a model airplane, perhaps a football. One gift each was all that my mother could afford, and Aunt Bea was careful not to make the other kids jealous by giving me another. Our secret was that we would go to the movies and the Automat one day during the holidays and then, like cheating lovers, we would go to the stamp department at Macy's, where I could pick out some really good stamps. The other kids would never know.

The present I found under the tree on Christmas morning, 1940, was a pogo stick. They had suddenly become popular and a couple of kids on the block had them. It was a simple pole about five feet long, with handles at the top and pedals about ten inches from the ground. These pedals were held in place by strong springs that would push up on your feet when you hopped around, so that you could actually get a few feet off the ground. With practice, you could control your movements. On the end of the pole there was a big rubber cover to soften the impact. The pogo-stick was a kind of wacky vehicle, and, at that age, we all loved motion. Skates, bikes, scooters, bumper cars and roller coasters. We even hitched rides on the backs of trucks, busses, trolleys, and horse-drawn wagons.

Unfortunately, all those sentimental fools who longed for snow on Christmas Eve finally got it. The sky was gray, the streets were white. Pretty soon, the plows would pile the snow in the gutter and over the parked cars. The soot in the air from coal and wood-burning stoves and furnaces would settle on the snow and darken it, until we no longer even wanted to touch it to make snowballs to throw at girls -- a peculiar form of courtship! I put the pogo-stick away until spring.

It was a grim winter, mainly because we seemed to be moving closer to the expanding war in Europe. Roosevelt had won a third term by defeating Wendell L. Willkie, an Indiana Republican. In March, Roosevelt signed the Lend-Lease Bill, which allowed the U.S. to provide weapons to democratic countries. I filled another scrapbook with headlines, many of them about the air-raids on England (the blitz) that devastated London and other cities from September, 1940 until May, 1941. There were many dramatic photos in the newspapers and newsreels. Houses collapsing in flames, factories flattened, smoke and rubble, air-raid shelters, and, through it all, the survival of St. Paul's Cathedral, its Christopher Wren dome a symbol of British defiance. There were also endless picures of ships sunk by submarines, the German wolfpack. A ship going under, its stern in the air, another in flames, men in the water slick with oil and sometimes also in flames. I tried to imagine being there like that in the burning sea. It was so horrible it made me tremble and sometimes have nightmares. I knew that my father had been in the navy, and in my mind I made him a hero in these awful scenes. I don't know why. He had never actually seen action. There was, in fact, no war on, and now he was dead. Perhaps all I wanted was a nobler death for him instead of all that madness and sickness, and my mother screaming in the street.

In the spring, I finally got to use my pogo stick. It was not easy at first and I was doing it all wrong, trying to get on the pedals before the thing was in motion. The idea was to start hopping right away. You had to get into the air and then land on the rubber stopper with enough force for the springs to push you up again. It required continuous motion, a bit like a trampoline, except that you were riding a gadget no bigger than a broomstick. Your whole body was involved and it was great fun, more difficult than riding a horse. Jump, land, hang on to the handles, keep your knees in place, push with your legs, pull with your arms, hit the ground again, push off harder, rise higher, leap forward, a long hop, and another one and another one, until you felt that you could ride the thing all day and guide it anywhere. In a few days I was so good at it that kids passing by or watching from across the street would stop to look and point. I was perfectly willing to show off. I could hop forward or backward. I could do a 180 degree turn in mid air. And I could hop with one foot and then the other. I

117

would pause to take off my sweater and wipe the perspiration from my face, and then I would mount the magic stick and fly off to somewhere over the rainbow, some Tahiti or Shangri-la.

"Don't you ever get tired of jerking off that broomstick?" said Lesko one day. His own imagination was too dark for simple, childish pleasures. He had already discovered a writer named the Marquis de Sade. I was reading *The Call of the Wild,* a book about a dog.

One day the big toe on my left foot began to hurt. I was sure it had something to do with the pogo-stick. I must have stubbed it, but I could not remember exactly where or when. I took my shoe and sock off and found that it was red and slightly swollen. I was sure it would go away, like all the other wounds we got from street games and horsing around. We had fat knuckles from hardball and bumps on the head from skating too fast and bumping into parked cars and iron railings. Twisted ankles and scraped elbows were also common. And none of these things were very important. We took them for granted and before long they went away.

A few days later my left ankle began to hurt . I pushed down my stocking and found that it, too, was swollen and red. Soon my right knee began to swell. Still, I went hopping around, feeling my heart race from the vigorous activity. I finally had to admit to myself that something was happening, but I kept it a secret. I didn't want anything to happen, and I didn't want anyone to know I was vulnerable. It would be a sign of weakness, just when I found something I could do better than any of my friends. "I'm king of the pogo stick," I told Aunt Bea.

"How nice," she said, smiling and frowning at the

same time. "But don't overdo it."

I kept my problem to myself for a few more days before telling her I had a swollen ankle. Her smile disappeared. "Let me see," she said. I told her only that much and I showed her. She felt it with her fat hands, the same hands that sometimes caressed me in the dark. "You know, your kid brother Al had something like that not long ago. Remember? They said it was rheumatic fever."

I had heard about it because of my brother, but he looked all right. She told my mother and the two of them agreed that I should be taken to a doctor, or at least to the free clinic at Mount Sinai Hospital. My mother called for an appointment from the phone booth in the corner candy store where a couple of my model airplanes still dangled in the window from thin wires. The earliest appointment was about three weeks away. In the meantime, she was told to keep me in bed and check my temperature twice a day.

They asked me a lot of questions and I had to admit that one day I got very tired and my heart was beating fast and *funny*. It was the only word I could think of to describe the irregularity. Aunt Bea took a folder out of one of her shopping bags and read me a few things, and then explained what she had read. "In other words, if you have had strep throat and scarlet fever, you are likely to get rheumatic fever. The symptoms are a little fever and aches in your joints. You have to be careful, because if you don't rest in bed, you might wind up with a heart condition, like a murmur."

"What's that?" I said, leaning back in bed against two pillows.

"I'm not sure," she said, "but it's really serious."

"OK," I said, "I'll stay in bed all day."

"That's not enough. You'll have to stay in bed until you can see a doctor. I don't want to scare you but you can die from rheumatic fever."

A cold chill went through me and I could feel my face turn pale. It was the first time I ever thought of myself as dead. In that moment, on that spring day, as I lay stretched out on the bed in the living room, the reality of death entered my life. It was an intruder who would be there forever. And from that point on everything was different.

By the time I was examined at the clinic, most of my symptoms were gone and my temperature was normal. "It could have been rheumatic fever," said the doctor, "and he tests positive for tuberculosis, but that doesn't mean much. He's probably been exposed to someone who had it, but that doesn't mean he has it. What about your husband? What was the cause of death?"

When my mother was nervous her face twitched. "They said it was pneumonia, but they wanted to do an autopsy."

"Did you let them?"

"No!" she said. "I didn't want that." Her eyes blinked rapidly.

The doctor made some notes in the folder he was holding, and he did not ask any more unpleasant questions. "It must be difficult for you -- being a widow with three kids. How would you like to send Robert to a sort of camp. It's called a *preventorium,* and it's really for building up kids from the city to prevent tuberculosis. It happens to be in New Jersey, in the country, but sometimes they will take kids from New York. He doesn't have to be sick.

In fact, they don't take sick kids, just people who might get sick -- you know, because of the tests. Three months in the country can't do any harm. And it might make things easier for you, too." He looked at me. "What do you think, Robert? Would you like to go to the country for three months?"

My expression must have answered before I could speak, because he smiled. "Yeah!" I said. "I would like to go. Yes, please." I turned to my mother. "Please, Ma! I want to go."

"He's not going to catch anything there, is he?"

"No! Don't worry. It's a wonderful program for city kids. He'll come back bigger and stronger. You won't recognize him."

13

The Magic Mountain

It wasn't a mountain and it wasn't magic, and it was nothing at all like the sanitarium in Thomas Mann's novel by the same name. It was the way I referred to the Tuberculosis Preventorium in Flemington, New Jersey, some years later, when Lesko was reading that book and told me something about it. It would be many more years before I myself would be able to read it. I found it difficult and unexciting and never finished it. But I liked the idea of withdrawing to the country and living a disciplined life that was beneficial mentally and physically. I got used to the daily cod liver oil , but not to the castor-oil punishments, maybe because I had read somewhere that Mussolini punished his political enemies by forcing them to take large doses of castor oil, a strong laxative.

Supposedly, all the boys and girls at this state-run camp in the country were at risk and had to be built up, even though most of them looked healthier than the average kid I knew in East Harlem. Tuberculosis was still a big-deal killer disease and, in old-fashioned medicine, was associated with poverty and malnutrition. None of us looked like starving Ethiopians, but we had all tested positive for exposure to the disease. It was a simple skin test that revealed an immune system reaction. Kids from New Jersey were allowed to stay for six months, but the New

York kids were only allowed three months.

The camp was really a paradise compared to Rev.Wilson's camp on the rotten-fish beach in Port Monmouth. The barracks were solidly built, much like military housing. The eighty or a hundred boys and girls lived in separate buildings. And each building was divided into two parts, one for the young kids under twelve and the other half for the older kids. There was also a common room with games and books and tables. In a separate building there was a dining room, an ofice, and an infirmary. The house mothers had rooms between the two wings of each dormitory. They were mature and experienced, probably between twenty-five and sixty years of age. The oldest was Miss Payne, who had been a missionary in Japan for thirty years and knew a thing or two about discipline. The youngest was Miss Jenner, who looked better in overalls than in her sweater and skirt. She was a real farmer's daughter, raised near Red Bank. She was assigned to the young girls. Miss Payne was in charge of the entire boys' dormitory, and seemed to be capable of reading their filthy minds.

There was a lot of racial and ethnic variety. The children were White, Black or Hispanic and had American or immigrant backgrounds. They were from places such as Jersey City, Patterson, Newark, and New York. Some were from welfare families with problems. I suppose that included me. But none of us were criminals or crazy or anything like that. There were juvenile homes for them. We were, in fact, very much like the kids in our own schools and neighborhoods. Maybe even better.

Since the Preventorium was open all year they had a schoolhouse of their own with three or four rooms and a little playground outside. What a change from the nightmare of P.S. 83! There were three or four grades in each room. Here the boys and girls were taught together in a very informal atmosphere. I attended school for most of May and all of June. When they closed the school down for the summer I was very disappointed. I wanted more. I had forgotten to look forward to a summer vacation, since I already felt as though I was on vacation. But there was still plenty to do and we were always carefully supervised. In addition to the dorm staff, we had an athletic director and two nurses as well as an overall director and her assistants.

Sometimes I thought nostalgically of Rev. Wilson stirring the pot on an open fire in the cooking shed, singing hymns and listening on the radio to the Brooklyn Dodgers and St. Louis Cardinals, his favorite baseball rivalry. I would miss his camp this year, and I wrote to Ida Moon to explain why. She wrote back and said that she cried when she got my letter but understood. And then I had this sudden image of her swimming around that pool as sleek as a human dolphin, and pursued by farm boys with huge penises like *ploughshares*. I remembered the word from Sunday School and from an argument with Weinberg over its meaning.

When it came to such equipment, I was still unable to compete with the older boys, two of whom were seventeen. I was placed in their group because in a few months I would be thirteen. There were no secrets about our bodies, since we all showered together under the watchful eyes of the housemothers. At least two were required for each shower period, but the older boys often attracted as many as four female guardians of sanitation.

124

Miss Payne was fond of reminding us, in her Christian way, that cleanliness was next to Godliness. And then she would go on to describe the steambaths of the Japanese. One of the housemothers who showed up regularly for our group was Miss Evans, a wiry brunette who sat on a folding chair with her knees wide enough apart to start a debate over whether or not she wore underwear.

One day, as I toweled myself, I bent over the water fountain and pretended to drink so that I might have a better view of things, but the light in the basement was not strong enough to confirm the rumors. For a moment she looked directly at me but did nothing to hide or expose herself.

Leroy Smith, a black sixteen-year old strong enough to pull a wagon, tried the same trick on another occasion and was given two demerits by Miss Payne for having a partial erection. She didn't call it that, but we all knew what she meant by "improper behavior," most of which occurred at night in the dark. She personally went out on surprise patrols to catch the older boys "abusing" themselves. The culprits were marched immediately to a cold shower, and second offenders earned enough demerits to "run the gauntlet;" that is, to run down two rows of boys, all of whom had the right to slap or punch the accused boy below the neck. Miss Payne believed in corporal punishment, and had established a system that included cold showers, slapping, paddling, the gauntlet and castor oil.

My own experience included some run-ins with the rules, especially in the first month or so of my stay. The day my group arrived we were told to strip and stand in line for examinations, shots, haircuts and baths. I didn't mind the shot, but I complained about how short the haircuts were, and when it was my turn I resisted. Miss Johnson, the nurse, who was a fertility goddess in all the right places, had to explain that it was necessary to make sure that hair lice was not imported into the camp. Eventually, I gave in.

Then I was given a hot bath. "Normally, you will take showers," she said, "but on the first day we have to make sure you know how to clean yourself." She scrubbed my hair with strong shampoo that burned my eyes and scalp.

"I can do it! I can do it!" I kept saying, but she ignored me and, as she leaned over the tub I could look right down her white dress at her wobbling breasts. My feelings were in such a state of confusion that I did not know what to do or say. I wanted her to bathe me and I wanted to see her breasts, but I also wanted to prove that I was a big boy who did not have to be treated like a child.

"Now, do you know how to pull back the skin and all that when you wash down there?" She held a washcloth in her hand. A layer of suds hid the parts of my body that she was referring to, but since I was circumcised I didn't know what she was talking about, and the expression on my face must have revealed my ignorance. "Well," she said, "do you know how to do that or not?" I shrugged my shoulders and she became impatient, but also seemed amused. "Come on, come on, stand up." I obeyed reluctantly. "Oh!" she said."I didn't realize --most boys have to pull back the skin. But all you have to do is wash thoroughly," and she did it for me, a little too roughly. "Like that," she said. I felt an erection coming on and sat

126

down suddenly in the murky water. She seemed to understand. "We're getting to be quite a young man, aren't we?" she said. "Do you want to finish up, or do you want me to do it?"

For years after that incident I scolded myself as a moron and an idiot for not taking advantage of Miss Johnson's services. She played a prominent role in my fantasy life, as did certain other grown up women and tall girls, including, of course, my first girlfriend and "Amazon," Ida Moon. My obsession with sex, however, became more general as time went on, and I found that almost any female human being who had attractive parts could excite me.

My own housemother was Susan Frommer, a tall young woman of perhaps twenty-six or so, not long out of college, not especially beautiful in the usual way. She had big feet and hands and was a bit awkward, but her bedroom was right through the pinewood wall of our sleeping quarters, a long dormitory with about twenty beds. There was a window in the wall, through which she could keep an eye on her boys. At night a dark curtain was drawn across it. I decided she was put in charge of us in spite of her age because she was big and probably strong. One day I found out she liked me, because she called me into her room to talk about my occasionally wetting the bed. I blushed. "It's nothing to be ashamed of," she said, "but it's got to stop. You're a big boy now, and Miss Payne is not going to put up with it much longer. If you don't find a way to stop, she's going to send you home. I will try waking you up before I go to sleep so that you can try to urinate."

That night about two hours after lights out she nudged me from a deep sleep and led me by the hand to her room. I was wearing only my undershirt and shorts. She had a private bathroom and suggested that I try to use it. I must have looked confused, because she took me into the bathroom, pulled down my underwear and stood me in front of the toilet bowl. "Come on, now, try!" she said, holding my penis forward so that I would not wet the floor. I was startled and suddenly awake.

"I can do it myself," I said. She retreated to her bed and waited. She was wearing only a cotton nightgown, and when she passed in front of the lamp I could see through it. I tried not to look and at the same time I tried to concentrate on what I was doing. It was such a conflict that I could do neither. I gave up and walked over to the bed on which she was reading a magazine. She wore glasses and looked over them at me. "I can't do it," I said. "Can I go back to bed now?"

"We'll give it one more try." she said. "Sit here and I'll get you a sip of water. That might help." The bed was cool and white and clean. As she walked to the bathroom and back I could see through her nightgown again. She sat down beside me and said, "Here, try this." She handed me a glass that was less than half full. My mouth was dry and the water felt good. "You'll probably have to wait a few minutes," she said. "Do you have any idea why you do this?"

"When I was little I had scarlet fever. It was after that, I think. I was afraid to get up in the dark, and in the winter it was very cold before my mother lit the stove in the morning. Then my father died." I said it before I knew why. She watched my eyes drift to an open box of chocolates on the night table.

She reached for them and said, "Would you like

one?" I looked around, as though it were a trick. "It's all right. Go ahead. Miss Payne's not here tonight." We both smiled. She picked out a chocolate and I watched her eat hers before I ate mine. There was a little chocolate ooze in the corner of her mouth that excited me. "You look sleepy," she said. "Maybe you should rest here for a while and then I can wake you up again."

"I think I'll be all right now," I said, standing up to leave.

"Are you sure?" she said. "I mean, if you're afraid of the dark, you can stay here with me for a while. I can turn off the light and we can sleep a bit."

"I'm OK," I said, trying to sound mature and independent. "Thanks for the candy." She came to the door with me, patted me on the head, kissed me on the cheek, and whispered "Good night." I was reminded of Aunt Bea and those early demonstrations of affection. Miss Frommer was slimmer and more attractive. I retreated but only because I didn't know how to advance. In any case, that night cured my bed-wetting, and I always thought of it as a miracle of some kind.

But new problems replaced the old one and I continued to rack up demerits in Miss Payne's book. There was, for instances, an adventure at midnight with a Puerto Rican kid named Manuel, who was about fifteen years old and talked constantly about the women on the staff and what a good time he could have with them. He especially liked Miss Johnson the nurse, who shared a room with another woman in the other wing of the dorm. "When it's real late, Mr. Dietz, the athletic director, he comes in to see them and they fool around. They close the curtain, but sometimes you can still see."

He persuaded me to come with him on this risky expedition. We went barefooted past Miss Frommer's room and past the sleeping bodies of the younger boys. In the shaded window we could see that the light was still on and we could hear soft voices. Through a crack of light we could see flashes of nakedness, but we didn't really get a good view. Manny moved closer and beckoned for me to follow. And then came the fatal cry in the night. One of the little fellows was having a bad dream. "Shit, man! Run for you life," said Manny and then promptly tripped over something and fell flat on his face. In another moment we were caught in Mis Evans' spotlight and we knew we were in big trouble.

My reputation was not improved by a showdown fight with a black kid named Cooper, who was thirteen and athletic. He imagined that I was flirting with his black girlfriend because I teased her about her nickname, which was *Moonshine*. I was secretly afraid of Cooper, but if I did not show up behind the barn at seven o'clock, I knew I would be labeled a coward. When I heard he was sharpening a nail file to use in the fight I nearly panicked. I was familiar with small weapons like these because they were used in street fights in East Harlem. When Manny heard about all this he brought me a nail file and said, "You got to use it, man! You can't let him get away with that shit."

Fortunately, word leaked out and both of us had to answer to Miss Payne. The fight never took place, but she confiscated the nail files and personally gave us each a dozen strokes of her bamboo cane on our naked bottoms before forcing us to shake hands. It was the most humiliating of her punishments, except for outright expulsion.

Afterwards, she sent Cooper away with a warning, but asked me to stay. And then she took me aside to ask me in a motherly way why a handsome, intelligent boy like me was so filled with resentment and stubbornness. "I was just trying to protect myself," I said. "I didn't want to be called a coward."

"Why didn't you come to me? We have rules here, you know."

"What good are rules, if he beats me up?" I said.

Her whole face tightened and her eyes narrowed in anger. "Don't be ridiculous!" she said. "Every institution has rules. Chaos is unthinkable and ungodly. Put out your hand." I obeyed and she hit me with her cane. The pain was sharp and I pulled away. "Put it out again," she said, obviously determined to break my will.

"No!" I said. "I don't want to be hit again."

For a moment she seemed at a loss. Then she said, "We'll see about that. I want you down in the basement, tomorrow morning before breakfast. I want everyone down in the basement." That could mean only one thing: *the gauntlet.*

I was determined to take my punishment like a man. I would refuse to cry. I would refuse to apologize. I would say nothing to anyone. I was not used to all this because I had never been punished before. My mother never spanked any of us. She was fair and reasonable. But here there was a kind of tyranny. Rule by fear. I was smart enough to feel the injustice. And silence was my best defense.

Down in the basement the boys were ordered to

131

form two parallel lines. Miss Payne described the rules of the gauntlet and then the nature of the offense. "Arrogance!" she said firmly. "Arrogance and pride. You must learn to respect authority, law and order, and the welfare of the group. In a democracy it's the people who rule and carry out the punishment. Now walk, do not run, between these two rows of your peers, and do not stop until I blow this whistle." The boys fell silent.

I took a deep breath, my eyes not focused on anyone, my thoughts all suspended so that I could not be afraid. The first blows broke the silence. I was hit on one arm and then the other. I moved on and several blows landed on my back and one on my stomach, more on my arms, even my legs. The boys were cheering and growling and preparing their fists, as if to show how hard they could hit. Not one refused when his turn came. Even Manny threw his punch. Later he said, "You were great, man. They couldn't make you cry."

But that night, in bed, I did cry, and not because the bruises still hurt, but because the boys all seemed to enjoy hitting me. I didn't understand it. In the several days that followed I thought a lot about what Miss Payne had to say. Maybe she was right, after all.

One day she came to me with a scarf. "Believe it or not, you earned this," she said. "You had enough good marks this week. I'm very proud of you." And suddenly I could see in her old face, not hatred but love, expressed in her own way. She believed in rewards as well as punishments, and from that moment on I began to appreciate those positive marks in her book, for attendance, for cleaning up, for my work assignment, which was sweeping the dining room after dinner. I became very

132

proud of that job and did it well. I began to receive points for all sorts of things, including reading books. I finished *The Call of the Wild* and then *The Sea Wolf* and then several Tom Swift adventures. I tried *Moby Dick* but found it much too difficult. The awards for good behavior and accomplishments were special scarves that could be worn during the following week, or special shirts and sweaters and badges like military medals. They were all designed to show the world your virtues, and I was completely won over to this kind of success. Before long, Miss Payne and I actually became friends, and she told me all about her years in Japan, and how sad she felt because America and Japan seemed to be on the brink of war.

There was a radio in the common room and each evening Miss Payne listened to the news and, I am sure, hoped to broaden the interests of her boys. Sometimes I sat with her. She was impressed with how much I knew about world events, especially the war. I told her about my scrapbooks and she thought that was a very admirable achievement. "Someday you will be able to show those scrapbooks to your grandchildren." I did not think of it in those terms. I just liked feeling connected with gigantic events in the real world. And there was certainly a lot going on that spring and summer.

On June 22, 1941 the two of us were listening when the news broke that Germany had invaded Russia, in spite of the non-aggression pact between those two countries, which was signed in August, 1939 on the eve of World War II. We listened in silence, and some other members of the staff looked up from their magazines or sewing. The voice of the commentator was grim: *"Even as the world awaited the Nazi invasion of England, the Germans were secretly planning this massive assault on the Soviet Union. The synchronized attack began at precisely 3:15 a.m. all along the 500 mile banks of the Bug River. The dawn was shattered by an artillery barrage of 7000 guns. The surprise attack did not give the Russians time to destroy their bridges. Panzer units poured across them, while the Luftwaffe, in the biggest air attack in history, caught most of the Russian planes on the ground, and are reported to have destoyed over 1200 of them, virtually crippling the Russian airforce. Their ground forces are everywhere in retreat as the Nazis demonstrate their dreaded Blitzkrieg, their all-out offensive."*

Miss Payne looked suddenly older. She kept shaking her head, as though to deny the truth of the report. "Hitler's crazy," I said. "The Soviet Union is too big, and the winters are terrible."

"Yes," she said, "but this means that the Japanese will probably join the Germans, and between the two of them they may be able to do it. Besides, it also means that we may have to go to war eventually against Japan. I was hoping that would not happen. I have many friends there."

"Why did you leave?" I said.

For a few moments she said nothing, as though she had not even heard me, but then she said, "It's too complicated. I can't tell you."

Her tone made we wonder. Had she been an American spy in Japan all those years? She would have been a very convincing missionary. And maybe she really was one, for all I knew. I never did find out. A few days later she handed me a new scrapbook. She had been to Flemington in her 1936 Ford station wagon.

134

Towards the end of my stay at the Preventorium I fell in love with another Amazon. Her name was Athena and she came from a Greek family in Newark. I couldn't even imagine her with an illness of any kind. She looked incredibly healthy. She was about sixteen, tall, full-bodied, with dark hair and fair skin. She had a boyfriend named Paul, who also came from a Greek family. Everybody assumed that they were high school sweethearts and would probably get married someday.

For a long time I watched her from a distance. Paul was the oldest boy in our dorm and a regular winner of morality awards in Miss Payne's book. Athena was in the girl's dorm, and I only got to see her in the dining room and sometimes on the playing fields. She often wore dresses that showed off her figure, her slim waist, her firm breasts and virgin hips. She was one of the few girls who wore lipstick. Nobody seemed to object. Manny claimed that she was the daughter of some state official, which is why she got special treatment. In my own opinion she was a real goddess and deserved to be be venerated. I could hardly talk to her. Whenever an opportunity came along I was struck dumb by embarrassment. When I stood close enough to her, I could tell that she was about six inches taller than me. I could not have been more than about five feet two inches at that time. The whole thing was too absurd, too impossible. I had to keep it a secret from everyone. Why I allowed myself to fall into these romantic episodes I don't know.

When it was almost time for me to leave, I had this insane desire to tell Athena that I was in love with her, in spite of the fact that nothing could possibly come of it. I spied on her. I learned her schedule and where she walked to and from buildings. The more I told myself to forget the whole thing, the more desperate I became. Finally, I decided to write her a letter. I wrote and rewrote, sitting alone under a large maple tree:

Dear Athena,

Please don't laugh at me if I tell you how beautiful you are, as if you didn't know. I will be going back soon, and I am hoping that you will write to me. If I were older and taller, I would tell you that I love you. In the meantime, I will miss you very much, so please send me a letter if you can.

Love,
Robert

Before I got on the bus that would take me back to New York City, I managed to put the letter in the main office. It was three weeks before I heard anything. And then it was very brief.

Dear Robert,

Your letter was very sweet. Don't worry about being short, because you have lots of time to grow. But even if you were six feet tall it wouldn't matter because Paul and I are very serious and will probably be together forever. Those months in the country will be just memories for all of us

Yours truly,
Athena

14

The War is Real

A few months later Pearl Harbor was bombed. The attack came as a surprise to most people. When we saw the newsreels in the theaters we knew, at last, World War II was real. Those were American ships that were blown up in Hawaii, and those were the bodies of dead American sailors. Our ships, our planes, our men! And President Franklin D. Roosevelt spoke to us like a father on the radio, calling December 7th, 1941 a date that "will live in infamy."

My friends and I went to the newsreel theater every day for a week to see the attack with our own eyes. For years we had played with toy soldiers and traded war cards without knowing what war really meant, but this was different. Most of us had turned thirteen or fourteen. We wondered whether or not the war would go on long enough for us to be drafted.

I first heard the news on the radio in our apartment. It was late afternoon or early evening. My fourteen-year old sister was at our church around the corner with her friend Thelma, whose father was the sexton. My brother, who had just turned eleven in November, was reading a comic book in the kitchen, while my mother was making supper. That was our immediate family. I was the only one who kept up with the news, and even I didn't quite understand what I was listening to, partly because it came as such a surprise. The first report I heard came during a ballgame and was brief. Another report made things clearer, but I had never heard of Pearl Harbor. I went into the kitchen and told my brother and mother. At first they didn't react. My mother went on peeling and shook her head as though someone had been naughty. I went back and waited for another report. My sister came in and changed the station to get some music. "Hey!" I said. "I was listening to something important."

"Why do you bother?" she said. "It all sounds the same to me."

"Yeah, and your music all sounds the same. They say that the Japs bombed Pearl Harbor and we're getting into the war."

"What war?" she said.

My mother came into the living room and said, "Don't fight. There's trouble enough in the world."

I turned the volume down and listened for hours to the constantly repeated reports. In my head I could hear bombs exploding and machine guns rattling. It was hard to believe that a country that made toys out of tin and houses of paper could have the military power to threaten America.

Later, I saw my friends. "We'll kill them," said Weinberg. "In a couple of months the war will be over and they'll all be dead."

"You're wrong," said Lesko. "Look what the Germans have done in Europe and what the Japs have done in China. I think we'll win -- eventually, but it might take a long time and we might all be drafted. Some of us might even get killed."

We were silent for a moment. "It can't last that long," I said, and we comforted ourselves with a loud argument on the steps of the library on 110th Street. We still thought of ourselves as kids, and, therefore, immune to adult dangers, but Pearl Harbor left its mark on us. It was, in a way, our first step into manhood, and we could feel that there was more to come.

Immediately after Pearl Harbor, men flocked to enlistment centers. There were long lines. We all knew people who were ready to defend America. There were older brothers and even fathers. Cousins, neighbors, young men from the church, our sisters' boyfriends. Before long, almost every eligible man in the country was wearing a uniform. Even Mr.Alexander suddenly appeared in a uniform and announced to his stamp club that he had joined the army airforce and would no longer be able to meet with the club. He was hoping to find a substitute, he said, but that never happened. He went off for a while to a training camp.

Then he had a leave and invited me to come to Washington D.C. where he was stationed. My mother asked me some questions to be sure of his intentions and then she let me go. "He seems like a nice man," she said, "but why is he so interested in you?"

I shrugged my shoulders and then said: "He thinks I'm smart."

My aunt, who always suspected the worst, said, "Well, you're not smart, and he's probably a faggot."

"He's in the army air force," I said, having learned to stand up to her.

"That don't mean nothing," she said. "There's plenty of them in the service, especially sailors." She laughed, revealing pink gums and large teeth. "Those pants they give them must be too tight." She looked at my mother who did not laugh. Perhaps she was thinking of her husband in his uniform before they were married, before the bad days and his early death.

She gave her sister a harsh look and then turned to me. "Tell Mr. Alexander that you can go to Washington. It will be good for you to get out of this neighborhood for a while and see all those monuments, and maybe even the President."

Mr. Alexander sent me a ticket, and my mother and Aunt Beatrice gave me some spending money, and I was off, wearing a tie and a jacket that I was in the process of outgrowing. Everything was new and exciting for me. The train seemed luxurious. There were comfortable seats that reclined, and there was a dining car, in which I ordered the vegetable dish because it was only ninety cents. It had a nice arrangement of vegetables with an egg on top. I was waited on by a black man in a white jacket, who seemed to know all my secrets -- that I was young and inexperienced and that I did not have much money to spend. He was very kind.

Mr. Alexander met me in the station and took me by taxi to the hotel, where I left my little canvas bag. He went over the list of things he wanted me to see. "We don't have much time," he said. "I think I'm going to be transferred again, maybe somewhere out west. I really shouldn't say anything. 'A slip of the lip might sink a ship.' Anyhow, I hope I wind up in Europe. In the meantime, it was too late for sightseeing, so we went out to an Indian restaurant and then to an ice hockey game. He said it was his favorite sport. "I can't follow the puck," I said, "but these guys sure know how to skate." It was the first time I had ever seen a hockey game. By the time it was over, I was very tired. Back at the hotel I went to sleep instantly and hardly noticed him in the other bed.

In the next two days we went everywhere. We saw the Washington Monument, the Lincoln Monument, and the Jefferson Monument. We walked along the Potomac River. He explained everything, especially the Supreme Court and then the Senate where we sat in the upstairs gallery and listened to a debate about a woman's army corps. "It's history in the making," he said, and I was very impressed with his knowledge and enthusiasm. I also learned more about his views. He said he believed in democracy and socialism. "What we need in America is something like the British Labor Party," he said. "What we don't need is Stalin's kind of Communism. And Hitler is an abomination. There is nothing we can do now but to kill him." Everything he told me made sense, and I began to feel myself absorbing his views as my own. He called himself an *agnostic,* and I asked him what it meant. I liked his definition and said, "I guess I'm an agnostic too. "Religion doesn't make sense, and yet everything out there is so big that sometimes I wonder how we can know anything at all. On top of everything else people are sometimes pretty stupid."

He laughed. "How did a kid like you from East Harlem get so smart. You have just put your finger on the central problem in philosophy."

" What do you mean?"

"It's too hard to explain," he said. "It's people like you who make people like me feel we are wasting our time getting an education. Let's get a hamburger or something before we take on the Smithsonian."

I couldn't tell whether I had been criticized or

141

complimented, but he had a pleasant look on his face. He wore glasses and had a hint of a double chin, in spite of his age. He could not have been much more than twenty-four years old. His eyes were deep set and he had a high forehead, which everyone thought was a sign of intelligence. I didn't feel that way because I had very thick hair and a low forehead.

He lectured me through the rest of my three-day trip, which sometimes made me feel poorly educated and sometimes made me feel that he thought I was worth the effort. I can't remember what I thought of myself. I know I was a slow reader and most of my friends read more than I did, but I felt I had some kind of secret intelligence. Maybe it was just common sense.

Before long, Mr. Alexander was sent overseas, and we began a life-long correspondence. He assured me that he did not qualify for any flight service and was assigned to a control tower at one of the airfields in England. By example, he taught me how to write a grown-up letter, and he insisted that I address him as Bob and not Mr. Alexander. After all, I was thirteen and growing fast now. I was looking forward to that summer, when I could appear in Port Monmouth and make an impression on my old girlfriend Ida Moon.

15

Another Summer

During the two years that I had been away from Wilson's camp on the shores of Cedar Beach in the shadow of the fish factory, Ida Moon and I went on writing to each other in the same childish way. We exchanged ordinary news and vows of undying love, even though we hardly knew one another and were both charging towards adulthood through the minefield of adolescence. Two years was an enormous amount of time for me. I had reached puberty and sprouted a few hairs here and there. I had discovered my mortality through a brush with death, and I had spent three months in a preventorium at Flemington, New Jersey. I had also been introduced to a larger world by Mr. Alexander, to whom I was now writing serious letters about the war and my own ideas. In the fall I would be moving on to high school as a sophomore, having survived the "blackboard jungle" of Galvani Junior High School in East Harlem.

In spite of all this, I liked to imagine that Ida Moon was my girlfriend, my sweetheart. It was a comfortable arrangement that might have gone on for years as long as we never had to see each other. It is the juvenile view of love, from which some people never recover.

From the very beginning, the summer of 1942 would prove to be different from those two earlier summers, during which I held hands with Ida Moon. For one thing it was wartime. We were not able to go to camp by boat, because New York Bay was a restricted area, patrolled by the Coast Guard and the Navy. There was a cable barrier across the Narrows to prevent German submarines from getting into the harbor. Later, we found out that, in fact, they did sneak through. And too often they lurked just a few miles outside and torpedoed our ships within sight of the shore. There were often pictures in *The Daily News* of oil tankers going down in flames and smoke, while blackened crew members struggled in the water.

I missed the ride on *The Keansburgh,* an excursion boat that sailed between Manhattan and the Jersey shore, going back to the days when there was a lively boardwalk at Keansburgh, and a clean enough beach to attract summer people from New York. I missed the fantasy of being at sea, and imagined myself as a sailor. I even had a sailor hat from the time I first went away to camp. I wore it again on this trip, even though we had to go by bus. I also had with me a pair of sailor pants, flared at the bottom and made of denim. When I wore the hat and pants with a t-shirt and a blue cardigan, I imagined I really looked like a sailor. But when I thought about it in the night, when I thought about really going off to war in the navy, I was frightened. I didn't want to fight and die, not even for my country. Not for anybody or anything!

When we arrived at our camp site, the canvas tents were up but empty. There were three large tents on wooden foundations. Usually there were cots with mattresses, but the owner of the place had stored things away, because he was sure we would not come this year. Later that day a pickup truck arrived and, in several trips, brought us rusty cots and damp mattresses from Mr. Fox's barn. We managed to set things up before dark, but I could not sleep that night because of the musty smell and the crowded tent.

In a day or so the camp was functioning as it once did, but it did not seem as orderly or as cheerful. Many of the men who helped Mr. Wilson, were now in the service. There were several Puerto Rican kids and some resentment from the others. The street gangs in East Harlem were getting larger and tougher.To stay out of them, my friends and I used addresses of friends or relatives to avoid going to Benjamin Franklin High School. Several of us wound up in James Monroe High School in the Bronx, a good school in a Jewish neighborhood. We could get there on the Pelham Line in less than half an hour.

The one thing that did not change at Wilson's camp was Reverend Wilson himself. He went on singing his hymns in the cooking shed and listening to the Dodger games on the radio. He had two sons in the army but never said anything about them. And he never said anything about the changing neighborhood, where his church was forced to accept new waves of immigrants.

During the first two days I did not try to find Ida Moon. On the third day, I washed up at the hand pump, combed my hair carefully and put on my sailor pants. Then I walked up to her father's store and bought a Royal Crown soda. I sat outside on the homemade wooden bench and waited. I don't think her father or mother recognized me, but I didn't say anything to them. I just waited around.

I was beginning to feel invisible, but suddenly Ida Moon appeared, smiling and tall and almost a woman. She was about a year older than me from the beginning, but now she seemed at least three years older. The same thing had happened to my sister, who at fourteen now passed for eighteen and went out with men in military uniforms. She wore Betty Grable hairdoes and makeup and had a boyfriend in the Coast Guard, and another in the army air force who was a twenty-six year old captain. To build the morale of our men, she sent out photos of herself in a bathing suit to a long list, many of them boys from the church. Ida Moon's hair was straight and parted in the middle and she did not wear makeup, but then she was a farm girl and didn't really need any. Besides, her parents were strict and would not have allowed her to flaunt herself shamelessly. My mother's attitude was much more modern and permissive. After all, she herself had gone to work at fifteen for the Telephone Company.

"Hello Bobby!" said Ida, her teeth gleaming white against her suntanned skin. She looked me over with a slight frown, as though perhaps there wasn't enough of me for a big farmgirl like her.

"Hello Ida," I said, suddenly frightened by her large breasts.

"I really missed you," she said. "How have you been all this time? You look great. You really do. Would you like to go for a walk?" She lowered her voice. "My mother is looking at us through the store window."

We walked up the road to the lane through the high reeds where we accomplished our first kiss. She reminded me, but I too remembered. "Now I can give you a proper greeting," she said, and kissed me on the mouth so vigorously that I pulled away. "What's the matter?" she said. "Don't you like me anymore? Don't you think I look nice? I wore my new skirt. We've been to Red Bank. And this is my Freshman cheerleader's sweater." She patted

146

herself on the bosom of her sweater, which was decorated with a large letter M. "I made the squad. I can twirl a baton and do cartwheels. I also made the swimming team."

"That's great!" I said. "And, of course, I still like you. I'm just surprised. You look so grown up."

"I know. When the Coast Guard guys patrol the beaches they flirt with me, but I don't even give them a look."

"But there are boys at your school," I said. "I bet you do things with them."

"Sure, but that's school. We go to the skating rink sometimes, or the movies, or bowling. But there's usually a bunch of us. I don't have a boyfriend. Honest!"

"I don't either," I said. "I mean I don't have a girlfriend. I hardly know any girls. My school has only boys." My confession was painfully true. My sexual experiences were limited to teasing and some stumbling attempts to dance at the church's "teen club." I didn't tell her about how often I had an erection that demanded attention, or glimpses I had of certain magazines about nudism that were lying around Lesko's room. He had an older brother, who had an intense interest in women. He was in the army and overseas already, sending back little blue v-letters about how gorgeous the English girls were.

We came out of the sheltered lane, which ended at an empty beach where there were no cabins but plenty of driftwood, seaweed, and dead horshoe crabs.
We sat down on a log that had drifted ashore during a storm and she took me by the hand. "I'm glad you don't know many girls," she said. "And I'm glad that you're jealous. That's the way it should be."

"Why?" I said.

"Because, if a boy is jealous, it means he likes you. And girls have to look pretty because they have to compete with other girls, otherwise they'll never get married. That's what happened to my Aunt Gladys. Her father was too strict and she never found a boyfriend. After a while, she was just too old. All the boys were taken."

She made everything sound so simple and clear. So why were my friends and I always arguing about God and sex and the meaning of life? Why bother? Ida Moon had it all figured out. And maybe women were smarter than men, after all, as many of them claimed. I caved in. We held hands. She kissed me again. Then I kissed her and it felt pretty good, so I kissed her again. She leaned against my arm and I could feel the softness of her breasts. After that, it was like my dancing. I didn't know what to do next.

"I've got to get back to the store," she said, but she didn't get up. Instead, she took my hand and pushed it up under her cheerleader's sweater. "I just want you to do that, because you're still my boyfriend and I know you want to feel me. They all do, but I don't let them."

She was right. I wanted to feel those breasts. They were large and warm. She managed to guide my hand into her blouse as she unsnapped her bra. My heart was racing. I was excited and embarrassed all at once. I wanted to leap forward or run away. After another kiss and a crushing hug, she resolved my dilemma. "That's enough," she said, her face flushed, but her eyes full of discipline. "We have to stop now or else."

"Or else what?"

"A girl mustn't go too far. Otherwise, she winds up at Katie's farm."

I frowned. I had no idea what she was talking about.

"There was this girl Doris. She was only fifteen."

"What about her?"

"You know! Don't you know? You're not that stupid, are you?"

I shrugged, as if possibly I *was* that stupid.

"I thought New York kids were supposed to be smarter than us, but I guess they're not. Maybe on the farm we learn from the animals."

Now she had me thoroughly confused. Katie's Farm, her friend Doris and the animals! What was it that they all knew" I had to fake it. I took off my sailor's cap, took my comb out of my shirt pocket and ran it through my hair."I was only kidding," I said. "Of course, I know what you're talking about. So, can I put my hand under your sweater again."

"Don't get fresh!" she said, and seemed to mean it.

16

The Enormous Typewriter

The first typewriter I ever saw was on the desk inside the store-front plumbing business in the tenement house where we lived at 157 East 112th Street, between Lexington and Third Avenues in Manhattan, an address wiped out decades ago by slum clearance projects that mirrored the bombed-out blocks of wartime cities in Europe. Many of the old apartment houses built for immigrants included street-level shops. On our street there was a grocery store, a cigar store, a candy store, and Greenburg's Plumbing Company, its name made of large gilded letters. In the front window, under the sign on the glass, there was a lonesome toilet bowl, enough to illustrate the nature of Mr. Greenburg's business. Beyond that, there was a large wooden desk, on which there sat an old Underwood typewriter. At the desk sat a secretary named Rose, who was, I later found out, also his wife. In the back of the store, and out of sight, there were all kinds of plumbing supplies. It was not these that interested me. It was the typewriter and the fingers of the woman who made it work. She typed very fast and without looking at her hands. To me it seemed a miracle of some kind.

I had been told from the time I was very young that my father was a printer, that he ran a linotype machine and worked for the Sorge Press. I never saw him perform his work, but I saw a picture of him when he was learning his trade at the print shop in the Brooklyn Navy Yard. He stood beside a large machine that, I was told, melted lead and made it into letters. He had also learned how to run the large press. From that time on I longed to be a printer, but the longing, I think, came more from my fascination with books and newspapers than with a desire to follow in my father's footsteps. I was actually more fascinated by the enormous typewriter than the pictures of the big press, maybe because it was real and I could see it and hear it and watch Rose's magical fingers dance on those keys.

I made up all kinds of excuses to come into the office so that I could see her perform. I would ask what time it was on the big clock on the wall beside the American Standard calendar. I would pretend to be looking for my mother or my brother or my cat. I would ask her to teach me how to use the typewriter. I would ask her to type my name, or just to let me watch her for a few minutes. Mostly she would ignore me, but sometimes she actually chased me out of the store. "Can't you see I'm busy, little boy? Go outside and play with your friends." And I would go, of course, but once outside I would lean against the glass window and watch her type.

My friend Weinberg lived around the corner on 113th Street between Lexington and Park Avenues. The public market stalls were on Park Avenue under the tracks of the New York Central Railroad, which headed north towards the Bronx and Westchester County. Weinberg's father sold potatoes and onions. In the basement of his apartment house he had a storeroom for burlap bags and boxes and a lot of junk. When Weinberg told his father that we were talking about finding a club room, a place to use, so we wouldn't bother anyone, he said that maybe, if we cleaned it out, he would let us use the storeroom in the

151

basement. Weinberg told us about this and, of course, we had to have a huge debate about why we had to be a club and why it should be in a cellar with rats and bugs, but no windows.

I guess I was the Huck Finn of the group, always dreaming up adventures, most of them impractical, like building a raft to cross the East River, which was notorious for its rough currents. I was the one who made maps of imaginary cities of the future, perhaps influenced by the World's Fair. And I was the one who wanted a club, preferably a secret club. But it was also just the clubhouse I wanted, a private, secret place away from everyone. Anyhow, I liked building things and when I heard of this hole-in-the-wall dungeon, I got all excited.

My dream was a bit dampened by our visit to Mr. Weinberg's storeroom. The cellar was dark and probably full of bugs. There were cobwebs. We walked past a furnace and a coal bin. There were no windows, and the only light came from a dangling naked bulb. The air was foul with dust and something rotten, probably his potatoes. There was mold on the old bricks of the foundation. Mr. Weinberg stopped in front of a wooden door that hung crookedly on its rusty hinges. With a large key he opened it. It creaked like a horror film. Inside it was pitch black until Mr. Weinberg lit a match and then a candle. "I should put an extension cord in here already," he said in his heavy accent.

When my eyes became adjusted to the place, I could see that it was a hopeless mess. There were heaps of papers and boxes and furniture that never got repaired. There were chunks of iron and burlap bags full of rags. And everything was covered with dust. "How can we use this place with all this junk in it?" I said.

He looked at me and pointed his finger. "First of all, Mister, it's not junk. But, second of all, it's got to be moved out of here. I got a better place for storage now. I made a deal. Never mind what it is. So, if you want to clean it out, maybe you can put here a radio and play checkers or something. With whitewash on the stone walls and a light bulb, this place wouldn't be half bad. Anyhow, you should clean it out before you make up your mind, and if you don't want it, I'll pay you for the clean up. What do you say? Strong boys like you -- you should do it in a couple of hours."

I shrugged my reluctant agreement.

"Not me," said Lesko, "I have a hot date with Dostoyevsky."

"With who?" said Mr. Weinberg.

"I'm with him," said Quintero, the Cuban. "I have to draw a picture of a girl."

"I don't understand," said Mr. Weinberg. "The girl is maybe Dusty Evsky? What? What is it that you guys do? What kind of a club is this anyhow?"

"They just don't want to work," said his son. "Bobby and I will do it."

And we did, coughing and spitting and cursing. It was a horrible job, but I was fired up with determination, a condition I would get into in those days that would drive me on into impossible things and into a rage if I failed. It's a good thing I never got too serious about the scheme to cross the East River on a raft. I would almost certainly have drowned. Besides there was raw sewage in the river. Sometimes, for amusement, we would lean over the railing and look for floating condoms.

153

As we removed things and swept up the stone floor, I tried to keep up my optimism, but it soon became clear that the project would never work out. Just as I was about to plunge into anger and despair, I saw some sort of machine shoved between two boxes. I shoved some newspapers aside and there it was --an immense typewriter, bigger even than the one in Mr. Greenburg's office. "What's this?" I said to Weinberg.

"Can't you see what it is, you schmuck? It's a typewriter, but it's broken."

"What's wrong with it?"

"How am I supposed to know," he said. "It's been here for years. My father never fixes anything."

"Does he want to sell it?"

"It's not his. He gave it to me last summer. You want to buy it?"

"How much?"

"Five dollars," he said.

I shook my head. "How about three?"

"How about four?" he said.

"How about three?" I said.

He had a pained look on his face, but then said, "Okay, three! But it's a steal!"

"I hope I can get it to work."

"So if you get it fixed what are you going to do with it?"

"I'm going to be a writer."

"Since when?"

"Since about ten minutes ago."

The club idea didn't work out. Lesko decided suddenly that he wanted to be an anarchist. He was going to buy an old coat and line it with explosives, like a

154

character in a novel he had read. "The only power an individual has, is his ability to kill other people," he said. "Then he has to be feared and respected."

Some people thought that Lesko was crazy, and at that particular moment I was inclined to agree with them. A few months earlier I thought he was a hero because he stood up against the toughest kid in the school, a Puerto Rican named Alvarez, who worked out in the Grand Street Boys Gym and wore tight shirts to show off his muscles. Everybody at the junior high school was afraid of him, except Lesko. They had hated each other for a long time before they actually fought. It was Alvarez who provoked the fight and said, "Meet me outside after school. I dare you!"

Word spread, a crowd gathered. It was a real showdown, a shootout. Lesko handed me his glasses and the other kids laughed. "Hey, Foureyes, here he comes." The crowd parted to let Alvarez through. He handed his leather jacket to a friend and said, "I'm going to teach this motherfucker a lesson."

In just their shirts and pants they squared off. Lesko was nearly six feet tall but very awkward looking. Alvarez already had that v-shape from his workouts. His belt was drawn tight; his pants were pegged at the bottom. He was about four inches shorter, but he looked strong. "Hurry up before somebody calls a cop," he said.

They moved swiftly towards one another and started to throw punches. Alvarez tried to box with his opponent, but Lesko had the longer reach and threw flurries of punches that kept Alvarez at a distance. He looked stunned at first, and then gave up boxing for street fighting, working his way inside and using body punches when he could not reach Lesko's face. Everyone was amazed at the fierceness of the fight. No one expected Lesko to last more than a few minutes, but it soon became apparent that he was prepared to go all the way. He had learned to box from his older brother Joe, the one in the army. I will never forget the look on his face. The harder the fight, the more determined he looked. Both of them drew blood. Lesko's hands were bigger, and he was surprisingly quick. He seemed to be enjoying himself. When the blood streamed down his chin from his mouth, he actually smiled. When he landed a hard punch, Alvarez staggered and pulled back, but he would not quit.

There were no rounds, no time outs or rests. They would fight until somebody quit. Breathing hard and spitting blood, Alvarez called out, "You had enough?"

Lesko did not even bother to answer him. He just came forward, as if for the kill. They threw more punches, but it soon was clear that both of them were weakening. They clinched. They held on like wrestlers or lovers. One could actually see that their respect for one another was growing. They were both good. They were both tough. Finally, exhausted, they both pulled back. "Hey, man, call it a draw," said Alvarez. "What do you say?"

Lesko nodded. "Okay!"

And then they actually shook hands. "You fight good, man," said Alvarez.

"You too," said Lesko. And they went their separate ways, surrounded by their separate friends.

One of the first things I wrote about once I got the immense typewriter fixed was an account of this fight. I also wrote some letters to Mr. Alexander and to Ida Moon. I even copied things out of books and newspapers, just for the practice. I started out using just two fingers, but before long I was using all ten. My friends and family were all impressed by my dexterity, and so was I.

17

My Atheist Manifesto

I had been thinking a long time about religion, partly because my friends were always arguing about it, and partly because I had been attending the church around the corner since I was eight years old. Now that I had a typewriter I could put my ideas on paper. Typing was the next thing to printing, and anything that was typed certainly looked more important than the material in the scribbled pages of my notebook.

I had decided to write a long essay on religion after a talk I had with Reverend Wilson in his office at the church. He had called me in to ask me why I was not yet confirmed as a member of the congregation. I should have given him some feeble excuse. Instead, I told him all about my struggles with certain doctrines that I could not accept. At first, he didn't seem to know what I was talking about. After all, I was only going on fourteen, and probably no one my age had ever dared to confront him so bluntly. I was probably trying to show off. Sometimes I even pretended to have read a book that I only heard my friends talk about. Most of the time, however, I did not quote from books in my arguments, just from common sense.

"First of all," I said, "How can anyone believe that God looks like an old man and lives in the sky?"

He looked flustered and took off his glasses. "Who have you been talking to?"

"Just my friends," I said. "Another thing that

bothers me is that God is supposed to be all powerful and the creator of all things. So how come he created a world that includes death and disease. How come innocent little babies die? And how come there are earthquakes and volcanoes and floods." I suddenly heard these things as they were said to me by my Uncle Babe, the common-law husband of my mother's sister. He described himself as a communist and an atheist. I did not mention him to Reverend Wilson.

"Not so fast, son," he said. "You are raising age-old questions." He suddenly looked smaller sitting there behind his desk than he did in the pulpit or at the summer camp in the cooking shed. "Many wise men have discussed the problem of evil, and the problem of free will. God created man in his own image and gave him the freedom to choose. At first he lived in the Garden of Eden, but when tempted by evil, he made the wrong choice. He challenged God's authority by eating the fruit of the tree of the knowledge of good and evil, something reserved by God for himself. Then Adam and Eve were punished for their defiance."

"But did God know in advance that Adam and Eve would fail? Did he purposely create them that way?"

Reverend Wilson's cheeks turned red and he shook his head so emphatically that I knew I had touched on the key issue. He spluttered in search of the right words. "Nonsense! Nonsense! Where did you get all this nonsense? I've heard it all before. These are the questions asked by people who are unable to make the leap of faith. Just close your mind to such thoughts and open your heart to Jesus Christ, the Son of God, who has been sent to deliver us from evil. If some of your friends are Jewish, don't listen to them. They all argue like lawyers, and they deny that Jesus is the true Messiah. I haven't got time now to go over all this. Come to church. Listen to my sermons."

"I do come, and I do listen. I like them very much. Sometimes, I even think I would like to be a minister."

His face relaxed. "Is that right? Oh, well, then you were just -- just --"

"Just asking questions, that's all. None of my friends go to church."

"Ah, now I understand. Just asking questions. And very good questions, I might add. But here, take this booklet with you. Read it. Study it. If you decide you want to be confirmed, I will give you the necessary instructions. And if you have any problems, by all means come and see me. In the meantime, make sure you get a lot of outdoor exercise. Good for the mind and the soul."

I was nudged out of the Gothic shaped office door before I could say anything but "Thank you!" and there I was in the late afternoon of an early September day, as unenlightened as when I started.

I went home and began work on my essay. I would not be able to think about anything else until I poured out my ideas on paper. It was Friday evening. I typed at the round table in the living room until my mother complained of the noise, and I typed all day Saturday and most of Sunday. What I said, essentially, was that God was not a person, though he is described as one in the Bible. God is really a concept, a word to name all the causes for all the things that ever happened in the universe. God is causation, not a person. It is pointless to ask *why* God made anything. It only makes sense to ask *how* something happened. There are scientific explanations for everything, even if we don't have them yet.

160

I didn't come right out and say that I was an atheist, since I was planning to give a copy of my essay to Reverend Wilson, and I didn't want to offend him any more than I already had. I softened my reasoning and language a bit to say, "God is the cause of all things." And I also said, "Why anything at all happens is a complete mystery." I wasn't sure he would like that, but I really believed that there was no logical explanation for the existence of the universe. My friends and I confronted the age-old question of whether or not the universe always existed and would continue to exist forever, as opposed to the idea that it had to be created at some point. And it was usually God who was considered the Creator.

Lesko tried to derail my approach one day by saying, "Perhaps there is no universe. Perhaps everything that seeems to happen only happens in our own minds."

"But how could we have imagined ourselves without existing," I said. It was only years later that I heard about Descartes and *cogito ergo sum*. He saw God as the first cause in a mechanistic universe.

Of course, I wasn't talking in these terms in my essay, but my juvenile approach to the big issues wasn't bad. At the time I was very proud of what I had written. It was about five pages long, and I retyped the whole thing for Reverend Wilson. I had not yet discovered carbon paper.

We had no telephone and I had, in fact, never made a telephone call in my whole life. When I was done with my essay, I just took the copy around the corner to the church. Reverend Wilson wasn't there. I knocked on his office door several times, until the Polish sexton answered. He and his wife lived in the church and kept it clean.

People said he drank too much. When he answered the door he did not recognize me. "What do you want?" he said.

I hesitated. "I have something for Reverend Wilson," I said.

"He's not here," said the sexton.

"I can come back another time."

"Never mind. Give it to me and I will put it on his desk." He pulled the envelope from my hands roughly and closed the door in my face. I was torn between walking away or knocking on the door again to get back my masterpiece. I decided to leave well enough alone. The sexton was the father of one of my sister's best friends, and I overheard her crying one day as she told my sister how her father had slapped her for something trivial.

About a week later I received a note from him in the mail. "I have read your essay. You have some interesting ideas, but I think you will find most of your questions answered in the Bible." I read his note over about five times and decided that he probably had not even read my essay.

18

Early Failures

I was always too optimistic. I was always dreaming up ways to improve my life and the lives of others. When I got a job, I thought about how successful I might be, how much money I could earn. My father was dead. I was the oldest son. I imagined that in a few years I could get my whole family out of East Harlem and into a nice apartment in another part of the city. I didn't dare go as far as to dream about a house. In fact, the only private house I had ever set foot in was the home of Mr.Alexander's family in Leonia, New Jersey.

In our deteriorating area I worried about my sister especially. She hated being a pretty girl in a bad neighborhood. Puerto Ricans called out to her in Spanish. The Italian guys whistled. There were drunks and creeps around. I thought of my mother, and how much she would like a nice clean apartment in a nice apartment building, maybe with an elevator and a real janitor, instead of the madman who lived in the basement and shoveled the coal into the furnace. He talked to himself and sometimes screamed in the night.There were rats in the basement.

I should have learned from my first venture that optimism can lead to disappointment. That was the shoeshine business at ten. With the right shoeshine equipment, in the right location, I was convinced I could make money. All I finally got was abuse and sore feet. At twelve I thought I could work in the summers, but I was too young to get working papers. You had to be fourteen. Then I heard from my friends that you could deliver newspapers like the *Bronx Home News* and some Yorkville paper. The man who distributed these newspapers had an old stable or shop on 114th Street. He was willing to hire boys with or without a bicycle. He would give them a little territory, sometimes only a few buildings, and he would hand them a list of subscribers, to which new customers could be added. My friends all decided to give it a try, which was amazing, since we never agreed on anything and most of them talked more than they worked.

We were sent out with a bundle of papers and a little notebook and pencil.If our customers were close to the distributor it wasn't too bad, because we could return for another bundle from time to time, but if we had customers who were around 96th Street, the outer limit of the distributor's territory, then it was eighteen blocks away. You really had to take the bus down because the bundle was heavy, but you could walk back because you had delivered all the papers. Even then most kids took the bus back because they had to pick up another bundle to finish their list. You couldn't make much money with just one bundle of papers.

I saw the problem rigtht away, but I could find no solution. I longed to have a bicycle, but that was out of the question. Besides, in that neighborhood it would probably be stolen while I walked up four or five flights to make deliveries, even if I had a chain and lock. Once, I left the bundle of papers in the hallway while I climbed up to deliver just one paper on the top floor. When I got back the whole bundle was gone. I was shocked. I could see someone stealing a bike, but what would they do with a bundle of newspapers, especially *The Bronx Home News*. I never did figure out why people in Manhattan were subscribing to a Bronx newspaper. The whole thing made no sense, and within a few weeks we all quit and spent the rest of the summer hanging out in the library and Jefferson Park.

When I was thirteen I was able to get a job as a delivery boy in a hardware store on 84th Street. I didn't have any working papers, but they didn't seem to care. With a lot of young men in military service, it was getting easier to find work if you just looked old enough, which I did. It was my first real job and I felt very proud of it. I had had a love affair with hardware since I was old enough to long for a hammer so that I could get the nails out of the wooden boxes I picked up outside the public market. The wood saw was a great invention, as were the screwdriver, the pliers, and wrenches of all kinds. The most amusing tool was the monkey wrench and the most interesting was the level. Between deliveries I checked out every surface in the store to see if it was level. I also liked angles and latches and locks.

I delivered everything on foot. It was a neighborhood of nice apartment houses, some of them fairly large with elevators and doormen who looked me over before letting me in. Sometimes I carried things in a canvas shopping bag with the name of the store on it, which brought a nod or a smile from the doorman. It made me feel grown up and one of the useful people in a nation at war. Some places had a service entrance for deliveries. I didn't feel any class resentment when I had to use it. In fact, I felt rather pleased, as if I had earned the right to use it.

In hot weather, all that walking took its toll. My feet tended to blister. I sweated through my shirt. I tried to look respectable, because it might improve my chances for a tip. Sometimes my delivery was somewhere near Central Park, in which case I did not resist the temptation to sit on a bench for a while or even on the cool grass. How wonderful, I thought, to be paid for sitting in the park. Twenty-five cents an hour and tips. Not bad!

When I had spare time I was given chores in the store, mainly straightening up the shelves. Usually, the owner's wife was there, often alone. One day, the phone at the end of the counter rang while Mrs. Kruger was talking to a customer. I was standing right beside it, but I didn't know what to do, because I had never actually talked on a telephone. I was absolutely paralyzed. It rang several times. In an annoyed voice Mrs. Kruger called out to me, "Answer that, will you. Don't just stand there." In another moment she could see that there was a problem. She rushed back and picked up the phone. When she put it down again, she said, "What was the matter?"

"I didn't know how," I said, completely embarrassed. "We never had one."

"You didn't know how to answer the phone? I can't believe it." She laughed. "Wait until I tell my husband. All you have to do, honey, is pick it up and say 'hello.' You must have seen people do that, if only in the movies."

I wanted to tell her about the telephone booth in the candy store, where my mother got the call from the hospital, telling her that my father was dead, but I didn't. I always connected phone calls with bad news. Practically nobody I knew had a telephone. I didn't tell her that either.

166

I just went silent and waited until she finished making fun of me.

The next day she said that her husband was worried about hiring a boy who did not have working papers. "He might get into trouble, you know. I'm afraid we can't keep you."

"That's all right," I said. I didn't really mind. I was, in fact, somewhat relieved. My romance with hardware was already cooling off as the weather grew hotter. I didn't like Mrs. Kruger, and I had the feeling that she didn't like me. Somewhere I had learned the useful habit of accepting things. It was not a matter of fatalism; I just seemed to turn off my feelings and walk away.

I did not remain unemployed for long. This time I lied about my age and said I had working papers. It was another delivery job. Aunt Beatrice had seen a sign in the window of a pharmacy on 76th Street and Madison Avenue, a very nice neighborhood, and reachable by bus or subway. I wore a jacket and tie when I went for an interview, and I was glad I did. The place had a wonderful antique look, and the two pharmacists who ran it were right out of an old movie. I was inspired enough to say that I was a high-school student, and that when I graduated in two years I would be going to college and then to medical school. They were impressed and hired me. I guess my all-American look, my blue eyes and blonde hair gave me the right look. There was only one awkward moment. I said, "I know how to answer a telephone.." Mr. Willard and Mr. Thorndike looked at each other and frowned. Finally, Mr.Thorndike said, "I don't think that's going to be necessary." My job, it seems, was merely to deliver prescriptions and collect the money. Sometimes I was asked to sweep the floor, but the place was already immaculate. There was a display of antique pharmaceuticals in the front window, including large jars with colored water, red and green.

Since things were slow at times, I brought a book with me to work. It was called *The Human Body*, a popular approach to human physiology, which had just been issued in a paperback edition. I was flaunting my interest in medicine. I was hoping that they would be impressed. Instead, they looked suspicious, as though I might have been reading pornography. Or perhaps they thought it wasn't proper for a boy my age to be reading such stuff. After all, there were diagrams of the naked body, male and female, and all the parts were named. One day, Mr. Willard said, "Why do you read books like that?"

"Because I'm going to be a doctor," I said.

"You're too young to know what you're going to be," he said. "Why don't you read some Tom Swift books or maybe Tarzan?"

"I read those, too," I said, "but I know what I want to be."

"I see," he mumbled, and added something lost in his mumbling.

Things went along all right, until an unexpected and unpleasant incident. I had to make a delivery on 94th Street and Park Avenue. I took the bus, delivered the prescription and collected seven dollars. I was paid in singles and stuffed the money in my trouser pocket. I did not carry a wallet for some reason. I dozed for a few minutes on the bus, but was awake when we reach 76th Street. Back in the pharmacy I discovered that the roll of singles was missing. I had no idea when or how this happened. Probably the

168

money just fell out, but possibly someone stole it because it was not stuffed deeply enough into my pocket. It didn't make any difference to Mr. Willard and Mr. Thorndike. They agreed that it was really too bad and they hated to do it, but they had a strict rule about such irregularities. I offered to work off the seven dollars. They said that wasn't good enough. Their rule was to fire people when this happened, but only after the money had been paid back by working time. I said I understood and promised that I would work long enough to make good the seven dollars. They looked genuinely unhappy about the whole thing, but they were men with strict standards, men from another era. I had to admire them.

19

Exploring the City

My friends were delighted when I lost my job, because none of them were very interested in working during the summer. They preferred to hang around or go to ball games and museums. We were all interested in the city and spent much of our time exploring it. We walked for miles, just to look at the streets and buildings. We often went to Times Square, which seemed to be the very center of the universe: the central place in the central city of the central country of the main planet of the only solar system that had human life and intelligence. The point could be argued, but that's the way it seemed to us.

We went to all the baseball parks, to basketball games at Madison Square Garden, to open-air concerts at Lewisohn Stadium up at City College, to operas and other events at City Center and Carnegie Hall, We saw Paul Robeson in Othello, and we saw *Gone With the Wind* by claiming to be sixteen. We went ice-skating at Rockefeller Center, where it was legal but not free, and in Central Park, where it was free but not legal. We sometimes walked all the way down to the Aquarium at the tip of Manhattan to gaze for hours at weird tropical fish, sharks, groupers, and electric eels. And sometimes we went in the other direction, all the way uptown to the Cloisters, a museum of the Middle Ages, as quiet and soothing as a monastery. Our favorite ramble was to the Central Park zoo and the nearby Museum of Natural History. We were fascinated by the animals. We stared at them and called to them. We threw them popcorn and peanuts. And we laughed at them, especially at the antics of the monkeys, who did indecent things. "If you did that in public you'd get arrested," said Lesko once.

"If I could find a girl who was willing," said Quintero, "I would fuck her in Times Square." He still had traces of his Cuban accent, which sometimes made his jokes funnier, especially when he called himself "The Passionate Spaniard," and described his sexual desires. He was already fifteen and, actually, awkward with girls. He felt rejected by them, and maybe even by his friends at times because he came from Cuba. He knew how much the Puerto Ricans were hated in the white part of East Harlem.

We were all adolescents and talked constantly about girls. I was the only one who had a girlfriend, but I was beginning to realize that she didn't count, since I hardly ever saw her and was about to go to a co-ed high school where I was sure I would meet plenty of girls.

Wherever we went in our explorations of the city, the subject was bound to come up. "Let's find some girls and have some fun," one of us would say.

"We could go to Orchard Beach or Coney Island," said Quintero, who had been working out and had a presentable body.

"How about the movies?" said Weinberg. "Millions of girls in bobbysocks are lining up at the Paramount Theater to hear Frank Sinatra sing."

"Yeah sure," said Lesko. "If they come for Sinatra, what makes you think they're going to settle for Weinberg?"

"How about the museum?" I said. "There are

171

usually some girls wandering around there."

"Good-looking girls don't go to museums," said Lesko. "Only girls with eyeglasses and pimples."

"Hey, that's OK, man, as long as they have tits," said Quintero. "Sometimes the ugliest girls have the biggest tits."

"Yeah, like your sister," said Weinberg.

"What? What did you say about my sister?" Quintero had a temper.

"Nothing. I said 'not like your sister.' I mean, she's not like that."

"Never mind what she's like. I don't want you to even think about her."

"OK, OK," said Weinberg. "Let's go to the Museum of Natural History. I'm tired of looking at animals."

"What are we going to look at over there?" said Lesko.

"Mummies!" I said.

"Dinosaurs!" said Weinberg. "I love to look at those big monsters. What if they were still around, roaming the streets of New York?"

"They would eat you first, you fat little Jew boy," said Quintero."

"Hey, watch your language. If you don't want me to call you a *spic*, then don't call me *Jew boy*."

"Well, you are Jewish, aren't you?"

"Yeah, and your sister wears glasses."

"So what? So do you."

"All right, all right, let's go to the museum," I said, playing the peacemaker as usual. "Maybe we'll find some girls there."

"How do you tell a boy dinosaur from a girl dinosaur?" said Lesko.

"I don't know?"

"The boy dinosaur has an extra bone."

I laughed, though I didn't think it was that funny.

At the museum, we stopped to look at the Egyptian exhibit before going on to the dinosaurs. It contained the inside of a pyramid, reproduced in detail, using some real pieces recovered from the desert. We had seen it all before, since it was a permanent fixture.

"How would you like to be buried in a place like this?" said Lesko.

"It depends," said Weinberg.

"On what?'

"Would I have to be dead?"

Lesko did not answer. He just pretended that Weinberg didn't exist and wandered off to look at some of the jewelry that was buried with the pharoah.

As we approached the large area allotted to the dinosaurs, we heard some female laughter. "Girls," said Quintero, as though he were a hound who had picked up the scent. He took out a little black comb and passed it through his hair.

"There they are," said Weinberg in a heavy whisper that bounced off the stone walls. The reconstructed skeletons towered over us. Brontosaurus, Tyrannosaurus, Brachiosaurus. The voices we heard were from three girls in summer dresses. Something about the Tyrannosaurus amused or frightened them. Their faces were tilted up, as though they were trying to see the beast's head. Perhaps they were interested in its enormous teeth. From where we paused to argue about our strategy, they all looked pretty.

173

We approached cautiously, taking cover behind the huge tail of the Brachiosaurus. "I bet they're from out of town," said Weinberg.

"How can they be from out of town without parents?" said Lesko.

"Girls are girls," said Quintero.

"You want me to ask them?" I said.

"I bet you don't even get an answer," said Weinberg.

The red-haired one looked over her shoulder in our direction. She was beautiful. Maybe they were from out of town, after all, I thought. The other two were also good looking, but were less animated, less talkative. Their hair was neatly parted in the middle and less than shoulder length, like schoolgirls in a convent or something.

"I bet you fifty cents I can bring back an address," I said.

"You're wasting your money," said Weinberg.

"All right, then, you talk to them," I said.

He hesitated and looked down at himself. "I'm not dressed right," he said.

"You weren't born right," said Lesko.

"All right, all right, fifty cents. Let me see your money."

We both gave fifty cents to Lesko to hold. Suddenly the whole museum seemed larger and I felt smaller. I had been boasting again and now I had to pay for it. I took a few steps in their direction, pretending to be interested in the creature they were looking at. The polished floors reflected light. Footsteps in the distance echoed in the large halls. A uniformed guard stood patiently with his hands behind his back. I wondered what he was

174

thinking. I felt strange, like a creature crawling out of the past, moving through evolution like a lizard, then a bird, then a beast, then me. I had been told often that I was a good-looking guy, but I wasn't entirely convinced. I knew I was better looking than my friends, but that was easy, because they were all odd looking, gawky, or fat, intense, a bit crazy. If I were a girl I wouldn't even talk to them.

I made my way along the bones, trying to look like a paleontologist (a word I had just learned about ten minutes earlier). When I was close enough to the girls, I pretended to be looking over the boney thing once more, but with a frown this time. "Excuse me," I said to the nearest one. She looked at me as if I had already offended her in some way. I couldn't back off, so I continued in a half mutter, "Can you tell me which of the dinosaurs this one is?"

She made a hint of a shrug and had the expression of a rich girl who didn't have to know such things. She turned to the red-haired beauty. "He wants to know what kind of dinosaur this is," she said.

The red-head was bright and willing, obviously the star student in their school, one of those girls who is always the first student to raise her hand. "Oh, this is a Tyrannosaurus. Most dinosaurs were vegetarians, but this one ate meat."

"Just like us," I said.

"Well, yes, in a way, but it still laid eggs."

I didn't know how to respond to that, so I said, "Do you girls live around here? I bet my friends over there that you came from out of town."

"How did you know that?" she said. Her eyes were very blue, and my mind was suddenly very empty. A

175

cloud of silence formed between us.

I was finally about to say something when one of the other girls came over and whispered loud enough for me to hear: "*Susan!* We're not allowed to talk to strangers. Remember?"

"I'm sorry," I said. "It's my fault. I was just wondering whether or not you girls were from out of town." I gave her my best smile, the one that said, *I'm a nice guy. If you talk to me I promise not to kill you or rape you.*"

She relented. "We're from Massachusetts. Now, come on, Susan, it's getting late. We want to see the pyramid."

"Oh, you have to see that," I said. "It's great!"

The two blondes walked a few steps away and then waited for Susan."

"I better go," she said.

"I can't win my bet unless you give me your address," I said.

"I'll give you mine, if you give me yours."

That stopped me cold. How could I tell her that I lived in a slum in East Harlem. "Do you know anything about New York?"

"Sure! I come here all the time to visit my aunt. She's my mother's sister. They're shopping on Madison Avenue today."

"Hurry up, Susan," said one of the blondes.

She fumbled in her purse for a piece of paper and a small pencil and wrote down her address. Then she handed the paper and pencil to me. I put down my name and then scribbled 89 East 88th Street. It was a lie.

I carried back her address to my friends and

176

collected the fifty cents I had won. They were very impressed. "Why didn't you introduce the rest of us?" Said Quintero.

"They are not allowed to talk to strangers," I said.

"Aren't you a stranger?" said Weinberg.

I felt oddly bereft. "Yes," I said. "I'm a stranger too."

20

The Great Escape

If we were prisoners in a movie, we might be making a tunnel in order to escape, assuming we could agree on the details, which is highly unlikely, but we were not in a movie, and all we wanted to do was to find a way to avoid going to Benjamin Franklin High School. Not only did we dream about getting a good education, but we had a strong desire not to be found dead in the Jefferson Park swimming pool, which was adjacent to the school.

Sometime in June, before the summer of the dinosaurs and the out-of-town girls, I suggested that I might use the address of my unpleasant aunt in the Bronx to find a school in a more civilized neighborhood. Almost immediately, all three of my friends wanted to be included in the plot. We did not like the idea of breaking up, since we had been together since kindergarten. We would have preferred Stuyvesant High School, which had a program for gifted students, but we had not submitted any applications, since all that we were advised to do at Galvani Junior High School was to survive. There was also The Bronx High School of Science and The Manhattan School of Music and Art, but we hadn't applied there either.

It was Lesko who came up with the idea of interviewing the high schools, instead of being interviewed by them. So we composed a letter that said: "We are a group of advanced students in a school district with problems. We are eager to attend a quality school with high standards. Your school has been recommended and we would like an appointment to visit you." The first school we sent this letter to was James Monroe High School, because it was in my aunt's neighborhood. It was a big school and I figured we could all use the same address. Weinberg was not convinced."Isn't it going to sound kind of funny that we have four different names but the same aunt?"

"What if she is a woman with four sisters who all got married," I said. "The kids would be cousins with different last names."

"I guess so," he said. "And then what? Did we all run away to live with our horrible aunt?"

"Don't worry about it," I said. "They probably don't even bother to check your address."

We felt very important when we received a letter from Mr. Hines, the principal of James Monroe. He said he would be delighted to see us and even gave us directiions. None of us had ever done anything of this sort and we were all very nervous. We wore jackets and ties and shined our shoes.

When we arrived at the school, we felt like dignitaries. We were offered help by a teacher in the hallway. When we said we had an appointment with Mr. Hines, he looked impressed. He showed us the way and then stood there for a moment with a puzzled look on his face, as though he could not imagine what we were doing there. The principal's secretary also looked a little confused, until she consulted his calendar. "Ah, you must be the advanced students," she said. "Mr. Hines is expecting you." She showed us in and asked us our names, which she then repeated to Mr. Hines in a louder voice. We had never been treated that way by *anybody*.

Mr. Hines was a small man with rimless glasses and a bald head. He shook hands with each of us and welcomed us to James Monroe. He had been the principal for many years and was obviously very proud of the place. He probably enjoyed the tour more than we did, since it gave him an opportunity to impress us, even if we were only students. Before long, I could tell that he wanted us to come to his school. Why, exactly, I don't know. He must have known that the Rapid Advancement plan required a very high I.Q.

"We are, incidentally, one of the largest high schools in the city and State," he said. "We have an enrollment of over seven thousand. He showed us classrooms and labs, the huge auditorium, and the indoor swimming pool. I had never seen a school this big and this clean. Our junior high school was built during the Civil War and looked like a red-brick factory. The wooden floors creaked, some of the window panes were cracked, it had no gym or pool. The walls were painted hospital green. Everything about the place was depressing. James Monroe, by comparison, had a wonderful atmosphere. It was bright and roomy and full of useful equipment. We paused at a window from which we could see the football field and running track. I had dreamed of running with real track shoes on a cinder or banked track with marked lanes.

After the tour Mr. Hines said, "It would be a pleasure to have you here as students. I am sure you will all want to go on to college, and I can asure you that we do a great deal to help. We have special advisors and very good connections. Last year we had the second highest rating in the city."

Suddenly, I understood what his interest in us was. He wanted to be number one, the high school with the highest percentage of its graduates admitted to college. We were all impressed.

We didn't bother to write to any other schools. I said I was definitely going to Monroe. Weinberg said his parents agreed to let him go because practically all of the students were Jewish. Lesko said he would give it a try because he had to get away from the neighborhood. But Quintero decided not to go because his family was against it, especially his father. "He hates Jews," he explained to us bluntly, "and he doesn't want me to go to a school that is so far from home.

In some ways this was the beginning of the end of our childhood. For the first time in our lives we would not be going to school in our own neighborhood. We would be meeting new people, making new friends. Monroe was very large. We would not all be in the same classrooms. I would go out for track. The others were not interested in such things. And beyond all that the war seemed to be settling into a permanent chaos. Day after day there were huge headlines. More and more death and destruction. The American navy defeated the Japs in the battle of Midway. The Russians and Germans were fighting a bloody battle for Stalingrad. England was still being bombed. U-boats were sinking our ships. The Allies landed troops in North Africa, where the Britsh had stopped General Rommel, the "Desert Fox." We began to realize that it would be a long war, and that we might eventually be part of it though we were now only fourteen or fifteen years old.

In the meantime, we enjoyed our daily journey to the outside world, even if it was only the Bronx, a borough about which we knew very little except for Yankee Stadium and the zoo. I liked the subway ride because, after a certain station, the tracks were elevated and there were things to look at, fading signs on factories in slanting morning light; tenement houses, hundreds and hundreds of windows, in which I sometimes caught a glimpse of the dreary lives of ordinary people. The facades were hypnotic. Sometimes, in the hot weather, a woman flashed by in scanty clothes or less. It would always happen too quickly to be sexy, except in one's mind.

I learned immediately that at James Monroe High School I was going to have to work hard. I was not used to doing serious homework or being tested regularly on reading assignments. I started out math in a blaze of embarrassment by flunking the first three quizzes. Our teacher's name was Klinkerfuss, and she meant business. One day, she asked me to stay for a minute after class. "Why is your work so poor?" she said. "You look intelligent, but maybe you're not. How are your other grades?"

"I'm doing fine in English and History," I said. "Not so good in chemistry."

"And terrible in math," she added. "Do you plan to go to college?"

"Yes," I said.

"And what do you plan to study?"

"I want to be a doctor."

"Really?" she said with a hint of ridicule. "Then you'd better find a way of passing chemistry and math. That's all. You can go now." She was ugly but she was wonderful and I *did* find a way to pass both courses.

In history I had a teacher with a slight lisp and

tobacco stains on her teeth. She turned out to be Mamie Wallach, the wife of a young actor named Eli Wallach, who was in the army overseas. She loved her students, especially those who had some political awareness and leaned to the left. Before long she had gathered some favorites, whom she invited to picnics and even to her home. She had no children. I was one of the favorites, along with a tall thin girl named Wilma Friedlander, and a short mousey girl named Jeanne Emmanuel. There were perhaps half a dozen that first year, which was our sophomore year, since junior high included the ninth grade. We learned a lot about American history, which Mamie Wallach taught with great passion and conviction. She persuaded us that the American Indians were slaughtered to make the West safe for exploitation, and she explained the economics of slavery and the real reasons for the Civil War. "And don't believe all that bull about *Manifest Destiny."* We gasped at her language. She was lean and tough and exciting. New ideas galloped through my mind. History came alive and I could see myself in relation to important events: the war, immigration, poverty, the struggle between capitalists and workers. I leaned to the left like Robert Alexander and Mamie Wallach, and I dreamed of a utopian future for America.

I had to take a foreign language, and was programmed for French, because I had taken it in junior high school. They could not have known how much I hated that language, but since I could not change my schedule, I faced the "guillotine" as bravely as I could. I remembered the look on the face of my French teacher in junior high. Every time I tried to read aloud or answer a question, he looked as though he was being tortured. If French itself

183

could be represented as a human being, it might look like Christ cruicified, blood running down his face from a crown of thorns. What I hated most was the way half of the letters in a given word would disappear up the speaker's nose and never reach my ears. How could a word like *maintenant* be pronounced *mntna*? What crisis in linguistic history could have led to this distortion? Spanish and Italian, after all, were fully pronounced. I hated also the constipated shape of the human mouth required to speak the language. Maybe the French were just permanently puckered up for an imaginary kiss. In any case, if I passed the French course, it would have to be through luck or divine intervention.

I fared much better in the physical arts. When tryouts for the track team were announced, I showed up on the football field, around which there was a neat quarter-mile cinder oval, the first track of its kind I had ever set foot on. Most of the boys came with equipment, shorts and sneakers, at least. I didn't know that this was expected. The new boys were divided into groups of five and were asked to run 220 yards in heats. Mr. Goldsmith, the coach looked at me. "Where's your stuff?" he said.

"I haven't got any," I said, as if I didn't really know what it was he wanted. He shook his head. "All right, just get out there and run." I was wearing the only shoes I owned aside from a beat-up pair of sneakers.

He used a starting gun and seemed impatient as he got us to the starting line five at a time. "On your mark," he shouted. "Get set." Bang! The gun went off before most of us were ready, but I was a quick starter. I was excited by a race, even over the cement oval in Jefferson Park, where I was the uncrowned king. I leapt out front and never looked

184

back. I crossed the finish line at least twenty yards ahead of anyone.

I walked back to the starting line. Mr.Goldsmith, who never smiled, said, "Where did you learn how to run?" He had a watch of some kind in the palm of his hand.

I shrugged, "In the park," I said. "Sometimes along FDR Drive."

He looked down at my feet. "You're going to ruin those shoes, kid. Go to the locker room and tell Mr. Severn to give you some running shoes and a uniform."

Gym was required and I always enjoyed it. I was made a gym captain after scoring high marks in a number of activities, such as running and jumping, calisthenics, gymnastics, and rope-climbing. I was given an emblem that I could sew onto my sweater. My mother did the sewing and I wore it proudly, secretly hoping that it would attract girls.

Speaking of which, I remained a shy adolescent at first. Gradually, I felt more confident, but still, for some reason, even the girls who liked me did not seem overly friendly. Later, I was told that it was because I was not Jewish and that they were not allowed to socialize with *goyem*. I was told this by Jeanne Emmanuel, the mousey but bright little girl who was one of Mamie Wallach's favorites. She was also told not to associate with non-Jews, but she was determined to make up her own mind about such things. I was impressed, and when she proved to be affectionate, I was pleased but did not know how to respond. If I was going to give up Ida Moon, I was hoping that it would be for one of the real beautiful girls in the school. Jeanne was short and flat-chested and looked younger than the other girls, because she also was a Rapid-

185

Advancement student and *was* younger. But she was smart, really smart. She read everything that was required and more. She wrote excellent essays. She even explained things to me that I failed to understand. I was intelligent but a slow reader.

By the summer of 1943, we had still not crossed the line from friendship to something more romantic. Part of the problem was our shyness, and part of it was the fact that we did not live in the same neighborhood. We didn't even live in the same borough. We never saw each another outside of school. I had not been to her home and she had not been to mine. I was fourteen and Jeanne was a few months younger. I was looking forward to the usual two weeks at Rev.Wilson's camp, but with somewhat diminished enthusiasm. After all, I had started a new phase in my life, and that camp was something sort of left over from childhood. On the other hand, there was Ida Moon. I didn't know what to expect.

It was an odd summer. When it was over I would turn fifteen. I had grown a lot that year, and maybe was as tall as I would ever get. I still wore my old sailor hat but with a new pair of bell bottoms. I made a more convincing looking sailor than in the past.

Everything looked and felt different in Port Monmouth. There was a Coast Guard station at Sandy Hook. The beach was regularly patrolled because there had been reports of men coming ashore from submarines. There were more dead fish than ever, and the stench from the fish factory seemed more offensive. There were fewer adult men in the camp, because most of the eligible men in the congregation were in the military services. And there were more Puerto Ricans than most of us wanted. The atmosphere in the camp was unpleasant. Even Rev. Wilson looked grim. His sons were overseas and had apparently seen action.

The biggest change of all was the country store that Ida Moon's family used to run. They had sold it to someone else and bought a house up the road a bit, a place not nearly as convenient as the store. I couldn't just go there and sit on a bench until she showed up. She didn't even work there. She had a summer job in town. That summer I hardly saw her, and what I saw was not very encouraging. We agreed to meet at the swimming pool one day, but when we got there, we found all her high-school friends, and she didn't seem to know what to do with me. She was polite but distant. I began to suspect that she had a boyfriend, but she said she didn't. Once, we got off by ourselves and took a long walk. She seemed incredibly grown up. I felt as though I were talking with an adult. She said that her family came originally from Germany and that some people were saying nasty things about them that weren't true. I could picture her in a wedding gown or driving a car or pushing a baby carriage. She made me feel young, almost childish again. Before I even got back to New York I knew it was all over, and thoughts of Jeanne filled the gap. I couldn't wait to see her again.

By my second year at Monroe (my junior year in high school), some students were referring to Jeanne as my girlfriend, even though we were both too shy to say anything of the sort to each other or to have any physical contact. I solved the problem of our friendship by making a joke of it. In history class I sat next to her and sometimes whispered amusing things in her ear. Mamie Wallach did not seem to mind. She actually seemed to be encouraging us. It was an amusing game that no one took seriously, except Jeanne. Eventually, I realized that an attachment had developed between us. I didn't know what to call it or what to do about it.

One day, Jeanne asked me if I wanted to go for a walk in Pelham Bay Park after school. She knew her way around the Bronx better than I did. The park was only a couple of stops further along the elevated subway line, but Jeanne had to call her parents to tell them she would be a little late. It was a big park with paths and trails, one of which led to Orchard Beach. Others led to picnic areas complete with tables and charcoal burners. There was also a bridle path where people rode horses, most of them from a rental stable.

We walked and talked. Eventually, I took her hand. I felt self-conscious. My hand seemed to be sweating, and hers felt limp, as though she was willing to part with it entirely. Eventually, we talked about our past experiences. Mine were few; she had none at all, having been watched over by strict parents. She had, literally, never been kissed, but she added, "I had an uncle who used to kiss me on the cheek every time he came to visit, but he died." There was a hint of a smile in those shiny dark eyes of hers.

I confessed that I had kissed Ida Moon a few times, which wasn't exactly true, since it was Ida Moon who had kissed *me*. I was instinctively boasting, or at least exaggerating. I wasn't sure why. Later, I realized that I talked differently to girls than I did to boys. It gave me pleasure to make them laugh, and they seemed to like my sense of humor. They even liked it when I talked to them in a more serious way. All this came to me naturally, and pretty soon my relationship with Jeanne flowered verbally.

In fact, it became a romance that was made almost entirely of words and innocent walks in the park, or along the Bronx River, which was closer to Monroe High School.

One day our relationship took a great leap forword. Maybe it was the unusual warmth of an October day, and the feeling that soon winter would set in and interfere with our illicit walks and conversations. Maybe it was just irresistible curiosity. In any case, I put my arm around her waist, which felt surprisingly small. When I was not struck by lightning, I left it there, without trying to do anything further for a while. It felt nice walking that way, and she also seemed to be enjoying it. An unseasonably warm breeze whispered in the still-green foliage that was doomed to die before long. What could it have been saying? The fall has always been my favorite season.We sat on a bench. Some pigeons landed near us and did their comic walk.

I put my arm across Jeanne's shoulders and noticed how white her skin was and how dark her hair was by contrast. I touched the back of her neck and she smiled, turning towards me slightly and glancing at my eyes. At that moment I knew I had to kiss her, and did, first on the cheek and then on the lips, quickly, lightly, as if I were stepping into forbidden territory. My mouth was very dry and my lips were tightly closed. The idea of the kiss was exciting, but not the act itself. "I'm sorry," I said.

"What for?" said Jeanne. "It didn't feel like much. About what I imagined. But it leaves a little tingle." She touched her lips with a small forefinger that quivered slightly. "Try it again."

I kissed her again, just as innocently as the first time. "There, was that better?" I said.

She seemed to be thinking through a math problem.

Then she smiled and said. "That was really nice."

From that day on we reviewed the evolution of sexual pleasure from the holding of hands to the stroking of sensitive parts of the human body. We explored each other physically, sitting on benches or behind large rocks, or lying on damp grass under weeping willows. Like Adam and Eve in the Garden, we felt, instinctively, that we were venturing into dangerous precincts, but the temptation was great and we carried on through jungles of uncertainty and across deserts of ignorance. The lack of real privacy made it impossible for us to take off all our clothes and go to it like guiltless animals. What we actually did was fumble our way through garments of one kind or another in all kinds of weather in order to find the warm human flesh and the eager parts. Eventually, we learned how to satisfy each other with our hands, even though we had not yet learned to part our lips when we kissed. I discovered, during these months of adolescent exploration, that the male's equipment was a lot simpler than the female's. It was easier to locate and easier to satisfy. We whispered instructions and revelations to each other, until we felt we were masters of the game, without ever having committed the awful act of intercourse, the thing that sent Sarah Fisher away to a farm and then, probably, to hell.

To make our little expeditions possible, Jeanne invented the Philosophy Club, which, she told her parents, met two days a week, Tuesday and Thursday, after school. Since I was an unsupervised heathen, I could get away any time I wanted to. Usually, we brought along a candy bar or doughnuts, and maybe a small container of milk, rescued from the lunchroom. These treats tasted wonderful beyond all logic, because they were eaten in secret places and

190

seemed to fuel the fires of our romance. At last, we had to admit that we were in love, and we had to swear not to share this information with anyone at the school, because word might get back to Jeanne's parents.

We talked a great deal for innocent fumblers. We were articulate and we read books that satisfied our curiosity about a lot of things from sex to politics. We evern talked about what kind of a future we might have someday if we stayed together, which, of course, we vowed that we would do, no matter what happened in the war or after the horror of it all was over.

It was Mamie Wallach, of course, who never let us forget what was going on in the war and in the world. She talked about mass executions, about Zionism, about the German defeat in North Africa and the American invasion of Italy. She applauded the heavy bombing of German cities, but wondered why we were so hesitant about invading the continent. "That bastard Churchill is allowing the Russians to bear the brunt of the war," she said. And she warned us that it would be a long war and that some of us might yet be drafted.

This was my junior year at James Monroe High School. I had friends who were seniors, some of whom would turn eighteen before they graduated. I was still only fifteen, and still confident that I would not have to go. The possibility terrified me. It was bad enough to discover one's mortality in smaller ways, but all this slaughter, the bombings, the atrocities, all the horror was more than I would be able to deal with. I imagined hiding or running away, but I never said anything to anyone, not even my friends. I did not want to be a coward, but I believed that nothing was worth dying for.

191

21

East Side Story

The Puerto Ricans continued to move into East Harlem, and other ethnic groups continued to move out. The Jews moved mainly to the Bronx, as did the remaining Irish. A few Russians and Finns survived for a while near the entrance to the Triborough Bridge and then disappeared. The Italians were still the largest group in East Harlem, even though they had retreated across Third Avenue. They held the line there for some time and dominated the neighborhood from Third Avenue to the East River. They could still elect Vito Marcantonio as their Congressman in the 18th District. He had his office on 116th Street, between Third and Second Avenue. Anyone with a problem was told to "see Vito." He was our man, our hero, protegé of Mayor LaGuardia and head of the American Labor Party.

Unfortunately, my mother was unable to face the trauma of moving. It was a kind of phobia that made it difficult for her to accept changes. Perhaps there were too many such changes in her early life. Her father and mother died young. There had been a fire in her apartment shortly after she was married. My father insisted that they move to Brooklyn. When that did not work out, they moved back to Manhattan, not to Little Italy in Greenwich Village, but to East Harlem, a move she always thought of as a disasterous turning point in her life.

Now changes were coming so rapidly that she could

not cope with them. Her friends in "the building" started moving. Ella to Queens, Rose to the Bronx, the Alcorns, Kruglers, Croteaus to various places. "The building" was a unit of community life. First there was the family, then the building, then the block, and then the neighborhood, borough and city. When any of these structures started to break down, people began to feel lost and depressed. It was a kind of spiritual chaos.

So there we were in an ethnic battlefield, but on the wrong side of Third Avenue. We would soon be the last of the old tenants in the building, but we still had a few friends down the street or around the corner. And there were the church people, who lived in Yorkville or other nicer neighborhoods. We still went to church and there were still dances for the 'teens and pot luck dinners for the adults. My mother's friends all urged her to move, to get out before the Puerto Ricans broke into the apartment or somebody got stabbed. When her friends moved out she visited them from time to time but less and less often.

My sister and brother and I also urged her to move, but we couldn't seem to budge her. One time, we thought we could force the move by finding a nice apartment. We managed to get together two or three dollars and started looking. We chose some nice streets in Yorkville and walked along them, looking at the signs that were usually hanging outside if there were vacancies. We spotted a 4-room apartment on 85th Street between Third and Second Avenue. A nice, quiet street in a German neighborhood. We talked to the superintendent and gave him two dollars as a deposit, and then went home to see if we could drag our mother out to look at the place. She made a thousand excuses to avoid going with us. She wasn't ready, she didn't have enough money, it was too far from her friends and some relatives she had on 105th Street. In the end we had to go back and ask for our deposit. The superintendent gave us the money and said it was just as well, since the owner of the building refused to let us have the apartment because he thought DeMaria might be a Puerto Rican name.

Things continued to get worse in the building and on the streets. When we were part of the Italian neighborhood, we could count on the older boys and young men for protection, but now we were vulnerable, even if my friends and I came and went in a group. The Puerto Ricans imagined that we were a street gang and kept their distance. Little did they know how gladly we would sacrifice our friends in order to save our own lives. Weinberg could neither fight nor run. Lesko could fight, but was only inclined to do so if he was personally attacked. Quintero could also fight, but he was already showing the signs of stress that would soon lead to a nervous breakdown. And since I could outrun anybody, I didn't have to fight. We often expanded to seven or eight if we headed for the park to play baseball or touch football. With Nemarich and Fusari and Fedorak, all a good size, we made a formidable looking group. We also made a lot of noise since we argued loudly about everything. Where to play ball. Where to stop for hotdogs or ices, who was going to win the World Series, when the war would end, and where to move when we got "out of this fucking neighborhood."

Most of the time we played ball in Jefferson Park. The field was rough and we had to bring our own bases, but there was a backstop and plenty of room in the outfield. Besides, other guys came there looking for a game. Sometimes they wanted to play for money, especially the

Italians. We didn't mind. A quarter a man, or maybe even fifty cents. Around the ballfield was the cement track on which I learned that I had speed enough to run on a varsity team.

At times, we went over the Triborough Bridge to Randall's Island, where there was a good field and a quarter-mile track. There were soccer games there on Sundays, but at other times the place was fairly deserted and also eerie, because there once had been a juvenile prison there, complete with a cemetery. A brass marker made all that clear. Along the shore there were heaps of rocks to prevent erosion, and the swift current of the East River swept by menacingly. Sometimes we saw rats in those rocks and longed for an air gun with which to shoot them.

We enjoyed exploring the island, which we could reach on foot by walking over the Triborough Bridge. It was a massive structure that linked three boroughs as well as Randall's Island. I found the height of the walkway disturbing, but said nothing about it to my friends. Cars and trucks roared by. The wind blew. Sometimes it started to rain. It was really a dramatic walk, and it gave us all a sense of adventure.

For a long time we felt safe there. We hardly ever met anyone else. None of the Puerto Ricans came because it meant crossing through the Italian neighborhood on foot to get to the bridge. One day, however, on a Saturday in the fall, we went there to play touch football and found half a dozen Spanish guys who were also playing touch football. They challenged us and we played for a while. They weren't bad, but we were better and were ahead after an hour or so. We were probably all between thirteen and sixteen. Suddenly, they started to argue in Spanish and decided to quit. We sat down in the shade of separate trees and made no attempt to talk to talk to each other.

After a while one of them came over and said to me in an accent, " You want to fight me for the ball?"

It was mine and I was holding it. "No," I said, "but I'll wrestle you for nothing." I didn't quite understand what was happening. He was brown and wiry with his belt drawn tight around his slender waist. I was a good wrestler and figured I had the weight and strength to take him. My friends and his friends stayed out of it and we started to wrestle, slowly at first. He was stronger than I thought and possibly older. Still, I managed to move him around and finally get him into a hold, from which he could not escape. There was no time limit and he refused to quit. I eased up and he broke loose, cursing in Spanish. We were both sweating and breathing hard. His white shirt had grass stains on it. I figured maybe he was mad at that.

"Let's go," I said to my friends. I suddenly felt that things were about to get out of control. I picked up the football and we started to leave when the guy I wrestled ran up to me, called me something in Spanish, and punched me hard in the mouth. I was jolted, and when I put my hand to my mouth I could feel blood and, on my tongue, I could feel the broken front tooth. I spit it into my hand and took out my handkerchief.

Some of his friends made a move, and a few of my friends stepped between us. Someone tried to take the ball out of my hands, but I refused to give it up. There was a lot of hollering in both languages. Then we heard their leader, the guy I fought, screaming at the top of his voice. He was holding out his wrist and the blood was running down his hand and dripping on the grass. He looked terrified. "You cut me with your teeth," he shouted. "*Coño*, I'm bleeding."

His friends tried to help him, all of them talking at once about how to stop the blood. Later I figured a vein or artery must have been cut when he hit me in the mouth. They produced scarves and handkerchiefs and started to tie up his arm. Meanwhile, my friends and I just walked away from the scene, ignoring the curses they shouted in our direction. I never found out whether he lived or died, and it was a long time before we went back to Randall's Island. I walked home with a bloody handkerchief half stuffed in my mouth and the tooth in my pocket.

22

Pin-Up Girls

With about fifteen million Americans in the armed forces, many of them in faraway places we never heard of, like Iwo Jima, and Tarawa, Anzio and Cassino, there was a lot of loneliness to deal with. One could hear it in the popular music: *Give me something to remember you by.* And *I'll be loving you always.* And *Don't sit under the apple tree with anyone else but me.* And *There'll be blue birds over the White Cliffs of Dover.* Sad songs mostly. Sad young men, going away, perhaps to die. The crews who flew the bombers in raids involving as many as three thousand planes at a time were expected to fly thirty missions before being sent home on leave. Of these crews about sixty percent never finished their quota. They were shot down. The glamour boys of the air, stationed mostly in England, in the European action, suffered staggering losses from German fighter planes and antiaircraft fire.

Wherever the Americans were stationed, there was a universal desire for photographs, pictures of wives and mothers, and high-school sweethearts, or just a pretty girl to dream about romantically, the so-called "pinup girl." Some were movie stars like Betty Grable or Rita Hayworth. Others had no name at all and posed for magazines or calendars. Many ordinary girls volunteered to send their pictures and letters to strangers in uniform, men who needed a pretty face and a sweet voice to boost their morale. It was the patriotic thing to do.

198

My sister and most of her friends volunteered for this contribution to the war effort, and they did it gladly. They took the pictures and wrote the letters and usually received answers. It was exciting for them. My sister was only fifteen years old when she started being a "pin-up." She looked great in her bathing suit pictures, and went on for several years, accumulating her private army of pen pals.

Inevitably, some of these soldiers and sailors had leaves and looked her up. It was very upsetting for her to ask these men to come to East Harlem, to the tenement house that was beginning to deteriorate in a neighborhood that wasn't safe anymore. She often arranged to meet the boys somewhere else, but if she left the building all dressed up she was whistled at. Sometimes, she had to put up with obscenities, in Spanish or English, or maybe a whistle or a vulgar kissing sound. She and my mother often argued about this. My sister wanted her to move to a better neighborhood and my mother wanted my sister to dress more modestly. "It's wartime," my sister said in her own defense, as if she knew anything at all about the war.

She went out with quite a few guys and then eventually had an affair with a Coast Guardsman. It was a wartime affair that did not last, in spite of all the romantic language and tears. Under the makeup and in spite of all her pen pals, my sister remained fairly naive and was really brokenhearted. Other guys pursued her, but I doubt that she ever felt the same about any of them.

Aside from her pinup activities, my sister's social life was pretty much linked to the church gang. By the time I was fifteen I was drawn into their activities, the most popular of which were the picnics organized by the sexton's wife, Mrs. Pollicek. Her own kids were a group within the group. There was a son named Al, a sturdy sixteen-year old, who later enlisted in the navy; and there were three daughters: Winnie, Thelma, and Dotty. My sister and Thelma were especially good friends. Harry Fox, who was leader of the Boy Scout troop, eventually married Winnie. Both Harry and his younger brother Fritz wound up in the army. There was an attractive, slender girl named Virginia, who liked to dance at close quarters, but was too puritanical to do anything else. Helen and Alice Krugler were part of the gang, until Alice got pregnant. Rumor had it that Ernie Goodhart was the father, and in one version of the rumor they supposedly did the deed in the choir loft of the church. It made a great story, but, according to my sister, it wasn't true. She had all the details from Alice herself, who was a great explorer when it came to naughty things. She was a large, lively girl with thick glasses, another one of my sister's close friends.

I enjoyed the church gang's outings to the beach in the summer and the cookouts in Pelham Bay Park, where we went far into the fall. It was the usual teenage fun, but I had grown a good deal and the physical contact involved in some of the games, the dancing and fooling around, did not escape me. Tickling, teasing, and playful wrestlng all had a sexual dimension. In any case, I became rather good at these activities, and, therefore, popular with the girls. The fact that practically all of the older guys were in uniform, many of them far away, also gave me a certain advantage. But nothing personal came of all this.

Besides, I was still seeing Jeanne, whenever she was clever enough to get away from her parents. The weekends, however, were impossible, so I spent time with the church gang. I actually learned to dance at the weekly teen gatherings, and to appreciate the music that went with it. Big band stuff. Harry James, The Dorsey brothers, Benny Goodman, and Glenn Miller.

At home, I still fought against *The Make-Believe Ballroom*, in favor of dramas, sports, and comedies. I stayed in most evenings, because it was getting too dangerous to go out alone at night. While my sister was out with her friends, building the morale of soldiers and sailors by dancing with them at Roseland, I sat on the day bed in the living room listening to *The Inner Sanctum*, *The Green Hornet*, *Grand Central Station*, *Amos and Andy* and *Jack Benny*. During the war there were no baseball games at night, but basketball was broadcast from Madison Square Garden. The New York area college teams were riding high: St. John's, City College, Manhattan, Fordham.

In the kitchen, my mother ironed clothes or talked with Guido, who was married to her cousin. They were all friends from childhood in the Village. Guido was an engineer who worked for the City in Manhattan mostly inspecting subway repairs. He often stopped by. His frequent visits bothered my sister, but I liked having him around. He was smart and friendly, and gave us a sense of security. He seemed to come and go at all hours without worrying about street gangs. When he and my mother argued, they often slipped into Italian, so that we kids would not understand what they were saying. Maybe they were talking about his wife, who was, I found out later, mentally unstable. Guido's aging parents had a farm in New Jersey, where he said he would take me and my brother for a couple of weeks in the summer of 1944. His son Aldo actually ran the place and was not drafted. Guido said that we could help with the harvesting of cow corn, which was stored in silos for the winter.

Now and then my sister brought home a guy in a uniform. She introduced him and we went through the usual questions about where he had been stationed and whether or not he had seen action. Some of them were willing to talk while we sat around the kitchen table. Others looked distracted and uncomfortable, eager to leave. Sometimes I wondered how far my sister went with these young men. In most cases, I decided that they were wasting their time. She was not the wild and reckless type. But she made a great pinup, because she had a nice figure and smile and photographed well.

My friends and I were all several years beyond puberty and getting desperate about sex. None of us had experienced the ultimate act, though Quintero said that his father had offered to take him to a prostitute, and I, of course, had my little picnics with Jeanne. They were welcome but did not stop me from looking at pinup pictures in magazines or at girls on the street when we went downtown. All of us enjoyed sexy films, though the movies were carefully censored. We liked Hedy LaMar, Maria Montez, and Dorothy Lamour. *King Kong* was a favorite of ours, partly because Fay Wray jumped or fell from a high rock into a deep river and rose to the surface with one breast revealed. The shot could not have lasted more than a few seconds, but I once sat through the film three times on a rainy Saturday just to catch a glimpse of that bare flesh. I also liked the giant ape. When he was on top of the Empire State Building and the fighter planes were shooting at him, I rooted for King Kong, but he was doomed to die. A tragic figure. It was Nature versus the machines of civilization. It was also a love story, Beauty and the Beast. Whoever wrote that script had a wonderful time tossing around symbols. My friends and I argued for hours about what it all meant. Lesko said that it was the story of Prometheus all over again. Nature destroyed by the intrusion of mankind and his ability to use fire to make things. At the time I did not know who Prometheus was, and did not understand what fire had to do with anything.

There were other moments in the movies when a bit of nudity slipped by the censors. There was a film called *Ecstasy* with Hedy Lamar. You had to be sixteen to get in, but if you were tall enough you could buy a ticket. It was a little disappointing after all the things we had heard about it. And then there were the movie houses along 42nd Street, promising all kinds of sex and violence. We were unable to get into those, and rarely had the money anyway. Magazines were easier to find. There were plenty of shops in the Times Square area, but the magazines were expensive and sometimes we were chased away before we got a free look. The best acceptable magazine was *Esquire,* which had pinup pictures done by Vargas. His skill at capturing the female form in a variety of fantasy studies for calendars made him extremely popular. But *Esquire* was an expensive magazine that none of us could afford. Once in a while we came across a copy in a used bookstore, only to discover that it was full of advertising and offered only one or two drawings or paintings by Vargas. I can remember seeing these pictures for the first time and becoming wildly aroused. Later on, they could not compete with the photographs of nude women in such magazines as *Playboy.*

One of the members of our gang actually visited a prostitute. Naturally, we wanted to hear all the details. For a long time he resisted our questions, but then one day he told us. He said that, every Sunday, his father dressed up and went to church. His mother, who was chronically ill, never accompanied him. One Sunday, he insisted that his son come with him to the Catholic Church on 115th Street. He said nothing about the prostitute, but after the mass, they went to an apartment house on Lexington Avenue and he was introduced to a woman twice his age with generous breasts and a bulge of fat around her hips and belly. His father told him to wait there while he went out to buy some cigars. "She is going to tell our fortune in the tea," he said.

The woman smiled and said, *"Hasta luego."* Then she asked him if he had ever had a woman. He lied, of course, and she knew it. She opened the buttons of her dress and showed him her breasts. He got so excited that he nearly came in his pants. She told him to calm down and took him into the bedroom, where there was a large unmade bed. "Don't worry," she said, "Your father won't come back for half an hour. You will be finished in five minutes."

Then she arranged herself on the bed without taking off her dress. She lifted it up to reveal nothing but her naked body, and then spread her legs to show him what she had to offer. He was suddenly paralyzed and felt like crying. She made him sit down and mothered him for a few minutes. "Your father is a very kind man," she said. "I have known him for a long time." When it was clear that his father was actually a client of hers, he buttoned up and tried to leave. She laughed and said, "Don't be stupid. What difference does it make?" In another moment he saw the logic of her question. What difference did it make? He was just one of many, and her business was to make men feel good for a few minutes. He allowed her to unbuckle his pants and to show him what he had to do. At first he could not figure out the jungle of her dark hair, but then she lifted herself a bit and said, "Now, can you see?" He saw, he came, he failed. She laughed and allowed him to try again. Within three more minutes he was done.

Whenever he told this story it was a little different, until the whole episode became a heroic performance, in which the lady actually swooned from excitement. The rest of us were an appreciative audience, full of follow-up questions. "Did she suck your dick?" said Weinberg. "Did you go to confession before you went to mass?" said Fusari, another Catholic.

23

On the Farm

The family farm was in western New Jersey near Pennsylvania. The area was very rural, full of farms and small towns. My mother's cousin Guido went there during his summer vacation, which coincided with the corn harvest. In the summer of 1944, he kept his promise and took me and my brother with him. For us it was a great adventure. For him it was a routine trip by bus, because he often went on weekends as well as during the summer. His parents used to be in the business of importing and selling feathers for women's hats, but after the first World War, styles changed and feathers were no longer fashionable. His parents bought the farm and retired to the country. After a while, their grandson Aldo came out to live with them. He was a great help and eventually took over and ran the place. He put in some modern milking equipment and a bailer, and bought a brand new John Deere tractor. When things were slow he hired himself and equipment out to work some other fields. This about doubled the farm's income.

Guido also had a daughter named Edith who came out during the summer. She was still in high school in the city. That summer she was about seventeen years old and very attractive. She wore denim shorts scantily cut from an old pair of bluejeans and a boy-style shirt with the shirt-tails tied in a knot under her large, firm breasts. I could see that she wore no brassiere, which sent me to the outhouse about ten minutes after I arrived. There I cooled out, browsing through the Sears, Roebuck Catalog, until I came to the undergarments. It was only the spiders in the outhouse that kept me from committing my favorite sin. Edith was like that farmer's daughter in all those naughty jokes. She looked as though she enjoyed exciting all the men, including the boys. Guido did not try to get her to be more modest, but her grandmother scolded her often, mostly in Italian. A few hours after my brother and I arrived, she forced Edith to put on a brassiere, which almost ruined the whole trip. She must have noticed me walking around with eyes and whatnot bulging. I lay in bed awake half that night, praying that God would send her to my room, but he didn't, which ruined any chance he had of persuading me to believe in him.

At dawn voices drifted into my room through the same window by which the mosquitoes had recently left, the window with the broken screen. All night long they kept waking me up and asking for blood. I started out my first full day on the farm with mosquito bites and bleary eyes. The voices I heard belonged to Aldo and his father. In a heavy accent the old man said that one of the milking machines wasn't working. "I guess we'd better get everybody up and out," said Aldo. I can't call Richie until about seven-thirty."

His grandmother provided the alarm clock, a big tin pot and a large spoon. For a moment I thought the house might be on fire. I rushed into a kitchen filled with the smell of coffee and was almost blinded by the naked light bulb that dangled from the low ceiling. "Do you know how to milk a cow?" said Aldo.

"No," I said.

"My sister will show you. Have a cup of coffee

207

and some bread and butter. You too," he said, looking at my brother.

Edie took us out to the barn. There was a chill in the misty air and just a touch of sun through a patch of woods. "Looks like it's going to be a nice day," she said. Birds seemed to answer her, but, for the moment they were invisible. She was dressed about the same as the day before, shirt, shorts, and no bra, but this time with a red bandana around her head. "I have to wear this," she said, "to keep the hair out of the milk.

Up close the cows were much larger than when I saw them from a distance. They stood patiently in their stalls. "Aldo says the machine is broken." I tried to sound like a young farmer.

"The machine is always broken," she said. "I prefer doing it by hand anyhow. The cows prefer it too."

I wasn't sure what she meant by that. She sat down beside a huge black and white cow with a loaded bag between its rear legs. "The first thing you have to remember is to always sit on the cow's right side. Otherwise, they get upset. "You take the bucket like this." She put it under the bag. "Then you massage the teats like this." And she went to work, as if she were dealing with four men all at once. I blushed at the similarity of the teats to a grown man's penis. The whole barn was warm from the cows and had a strong odor of sour milk and damp hay. "Now watch closely," she said. "This is important. You have to get the feel of it. You have to start to squeeze near the top and strip the teat downward to make sure you force the milk through. Watch!" She started milking the cow, who seemed a little restless. She worked on two teats at a time, one with each hand and in a steady rhythm, so that the milk that came out made a sound in the metal bucket: one, two, one two. I got an erection as I stood beside her and could only hope that she didn't notice it. Or maybe I wanted her to. That was a much better idea.

My fantasy ended abruptly when she said, "Okay, sit down. Give it a try. You have nice big hands." I paused to look at my own hands, and then tried to imitate what she had done. Some milk came out but it missed the pail and hit me in the leg. "That's all right, don't worry about it," she said. "Keep going." She put her hands on mine to show me how it was done. To do this she had to press her breasts against my back with her face close to mine. "Now don't squeeze too hard. Let the milk come through. That's right. Like that. Yes, that's it, just like that. A little harder. A little quicker. Get in a rhythm. I could feel her warm breath against my cheek.

Suddenly, it occurred to me that she might be enjoying herself. I lifted my head suddenly and hit her in the nose. At the same time I knocked over the bucket with my left foot and lost my balance. To keep from falling I held on to the two teats, as though there were handles or ropes. The milk squirted everywhere -- on me, on Edith, on the hay, even on my brother. The cow let out a moo of disapproval and shifted her weight. Edith fell down laughing. I got up to help her, but all I managed to do was to knock over the stool. Edith lay there in the hay with a big smile on her face and her legs parted, as though she was waiting for me to jump on her. My naive brother helped her to her feet, for which I have never forgiven him.

At that point Edith's grandmother walked in with a big stick in her hand. "What happened?" she said.

"Blue Eyes tried to kick me," said Edith. "She

209

knocked over the pail and everything. She must be afraid of these guys."

"Sonofabitch!" said the old lady in English, and whacked the cow's hindquarters. Then she turned to Edith. "Now, you, go up to the house and get dressed before I show you the stick. And you two boys, follow me. Come on, come on!" Within three minutes, she had us milking cows like experts. Fear is a great motivator and it knows no language.

I had the typical New Yorker's view of country boys. We called them *hicks* or *yokels* and assumed that city boys were smarter and better educated and had more fun and advantages. After too many steamy nights in East Harlem and two weeks in the country, my preference for the city was severely challenged. I liked the silence of the morning, the misty fields, the circling hawks and crows. I even liked the hard physical work and the feeling of exhaustion after lifting corn stalks onto the flatbed truck all day long as it crept up and down the rows. And I liked the feeling of accomplishment when the conveyor belt carried the stalks into the chopper and then up a chute into the silo. Above all, I enjoyed learning how to drive the old truck and even the new tractor. What a sense of power to be behind the wheel of a large machine!

The presence of large living creatures was a reminder that we all belonged to the great reservoir of life. There were cows and horses, cats and dogs, chickens and geese. The horses were old like Guido's father, who had used them for plowing until the machines came. Now they were fat, fly-bitten and stubborn.

One day, the old man said to me, "Come on, I want to show you how smart my black horse is. He'll do

210

anything I tell him to do." We went into a small paddock. The old man picked up a piece of wood, about the size of a baseball bat. "Watch this!" he said and went up to the horse and hit him on the head right between the eyes.

I was startled and upset. "Hey, why did you do that? I thought you said that he would do anything you wanted him to do."

"Yes," he said, "but before that I have to get his attention."

On the day we were supposed to leave, I got up early and walked around the place. I thought about how wonderful it would be to own land, a piece of the globe, which in turn was a piece of the solar system and ultimately a piece of the universe, going back to the beginning of time. There were about two hundred acres here. I stooped down to pick up a handful of soil. It felt cool and damp in the morning air. I walked toward the silo and in the slight breeze I suddenly caught the smell of cut corn that was now settling in and generating its own heat. In that moment it was earthy perfume to me, and I thought of the schemes I kept dreaming up for getting out of East Harlem.

Every time I went anywhere I considered staying there. How would I earn a living? Where would I live? I wanted to work in Ida Moon's store in Port Monmouth. I even asked her father about it once. He considered it for a moment or two because the young man who worked for him had gone off to war right out of high school. Then he said. "I don't think you're old enough to drive the pickup." When we came to camp on the Keansburgh, I wanted to work on boats, maybe that one, maybe a freighter. And in

Asbury Park, I thought I could get a job running the ferris wheel or the merry-go-round. It didn't look all that hard. The kid who ran the bumper cars wasn't much older than me. When I went to Washington to see Mr. Alexander, I tried to imagine how it would be to work for the railroad. And, as a spectator in the Senate, I thought being a page would be a great way to start a brilliant career in government, a lot easier than what Abraham Lincoln had to do. This time I thought of asking Aldo about staying on to help out, and maybe finishing up high school in Flemington, but then I thought of Jeanne and how disappointed and hurt she would be.

I would be entering my senior year at James Monroe High School, and after that--well, I would have to talk to Mr. Alexander. He had told me, more than once, that when it came time to go to college he might be able to help me. On the bus ride back to New York I sat by a window and watched the world go by, dozing, day-dreaming, remembering Edith and the cow and the spiders in the outhouse.

24

First Stories

I had an English teacher named Mr.Barber who walked with a limp and was not eligible for the draft. Perhaps he was also a bit old, but I couldn't tell. He was tall and thin and .wor a mustache. There was only a hint of gray in his hair. He loved literature, and he thought we might appreciate it more if we tried to write poetry and short stories. I liked the idea, but I was way ahead of him and the whole class because I had been writing things since I got the giant typewriter. I had about ten pages of poems of one kind or another. I counted the beat on my fingers, and I was very good at rhymes. I had also written some simple stories and passages of description, just to get the feel of fiction. I didn't have to read very much. It all seemed to come to me naturally. I remembered my mother's account of how I started to talk. I didn't start early, but then I spoke a first sentence that was perfectly constructed. "What's all that paraphernalia?" I said, looking at a heap of things on a chair. She was astounded and told all her friends what had happened. None of them believed her, of course. Even I didn't believe her at first, but when I started writing stories, I realized that she had told the truth.

When Mr. Barber read my first story, he told me to stay after class. He asked me what book I had copied it from. I was offended, but I also felt guilty,because it was a story I had already written before the assignment was given. It was called *Le Chemin de Fer,* "The Railroad." He listened very carefully to my confession and to my answers to all his questions. Why did I use a French title? I told him that I liked the sound of it when I first heard it in a French class in junior high school. And I liked the fact that its literal meaning was "road of iron." It was the title, I said, that gave me the idea for the story. It was also my trip to Washington D.C. that made me think of life as a trip on a railroad, with the various events and places speeding past, so that it was hard to tell which was moving, the train or the world outside.

My idea was to have a passenger see things outside the window of the train that corresponded to episodes in his life. The final episode he saw would be the arrival at some destination. A stranger would get off the train and try to cross the tracks unaware that another train was coming down the track and would certainly kill him. He wakes as if from a dream and then, in the real world, he arrives at his station and starts to cross the tracks. His dream world and real world converge, but too late to save him from what he had foreseen.

Mr. Barber was astounded, not only by my story, but my articulate explanation. Before praising me too highly, he asked me to write another story for this assignment, which I thought was only fair, since the first one had already been written some time ago. The new story was called "Crime and Punishment." I had never heard of Dostoevsky or his novel. My story had a contemporary setting and was about a man who committed a crime and could not keep himself from returning to the scene, as if he wanted to be caught and punished. I thought it was a pretty neat idea and an obvious title. I was astounded when

Mr. Barber told me that a Russian writer named Dostoevsky had written a novel with that title. "I really don't know what to do with you," he said. "You're either a brilliant writer or a clever cheater."

"Why would I want to hand in somebody else's writing," I said, "when my own is so good?"

He squinted as though he was trying to look right through me. "I am inclined to believe you, but I'm not going to grade these stories until I see more of your work. Our next assignment will be to write a short play. Do you think you can do that?"

"I guess so," I said, "I've seen a couple of plays, but I've never written one."

"What have you seen?"

"*Othello*, with Paul Robeson."

His eyebrows arched in approval. "Very good! What else?"

"*Winterset.* I can't remember who wrote it."

"What else?"

"Do movies count?" I said.

"They can't do any harm, but you have to remember that a play is meant for the stage. There's a limit to what you can do."

"Yeah, I get it," I said. "Where do you want me to write this play? At home or in class, or maybe after class?"

He looked flustered. "I didn't mean to doubt you. In fact, I'm beginning to think that you're a natural."

"Once I get an idea, I can write it very quickly," I said.

"All right, then, give me a one-act play by Monday. It doesn't have to be very long."

I gave it to him the next day, which was Friday. He

shook his head in disbelief. "I had to stay up until midnight," I said. "Does it count if you look something up in the encyclopedia? The play is about two brothers in the Spanish Civil War. I read a little about it in the library and then I figured if the brothers were on opposite sides and wound up fighting against each other, that it would be a good idea for a play. The real point, of course, is that war is stupid!"

"Well, that one certainly was," he said. Later on, I found out that he was a real left-winger, like Mamie Wallach. At the end of the term, he encouraged me to continue writing. I said nothing could stop me, unless I got hit by a train. He laughed, remembering the first story I had shown him.

That year, I read more and had certain revelations about the craft of writing. There was more to it than I imagined, and every now and then something would become very clear. One day I was trying to describe the trolley cars that went by on Third Avenue. They could be driven from both ends and they could go forward and backward. When they passed each other on Third Avenue they looked as though they were one train stretching out, until daylight appeared to separate them. What struck me like lightning was *imagery*. I suddenly saw that words could evoke images. It was like painting with words. *Storm clouds grew like giant mushrooms and filled the sky.* I didn't know the technical name for it, but I knew why I did it, and once I did it, I would always be able to do it again.

Another time I was fascinated with faces. I clipped pictures out of magazines and newspapers and pasted them on pieces of cardboard, so I could study them. I tried to think of ten ways to describe human hair and twenty ways

216

to describe eyes and thirty ways to describe how people move, and so on.

I was fascinated by writing, but I never thought of it as something you could study in college. My dream of becoming a doctor was becoming a little hazy, but I didn't know what else I could reasonably major in, especially since I didn't even know what college I would be allowed to attend. Journalism, maybe, but that seemed rather flimsy. I mean, what was there to study? All one had to do was to describe the war or write about how terrible the world was in every imaginable way. To do that day in and day out did not strike me as a joyful or useful occupation. Actually, I didn't know much about how writers made their living, and then, later on, I found out that many of them didn't.

It was my senior year and I drifted into the fall without making any plans. A letter from Mr. Alexander reminded me that I should be applying to colleges. He said that he was back in Washington D.C. after his long tour of duty in the Army Air Force and that he would be coming home to visit his parents in Leonia. He gave me some dates and a number to call.

On a mild Saturday in October, I waited on the steps of the New York Public Library between the stone lions, a favorite meeting place in New York, like "under the arch in Washington Square Park." I sat there, watching the people and traffic go by on Fifth Avenue, and I felt almost invisible, because I knew no one and was connected to none of the buildings, none of the offices, none of the private cars or the trucks with signs that anounced their business in the world or at least in New York City. It was a familiar feeling, and not unpleasant, with white puffs of clouds in the avenues of the blue sky above the canyons of the city.

Mr. Alexander was still in uniform, and still only a sergeant. I had expected him to be an officer. My sister had been out with some guys who were captains or majors in their early twenties. Mostly Air Force men, who moved up quickly, if they didn't get shot down. I saw him before he saw me. He looked slimmer, older. He hugged a newspaper and a book to his khaki shirt, on which there were some ribbons pinned for service overseas. If he were in civilian clothes he'd look like a college professor, which is what he was going to be after the war, either in Economics or in Latin American History. By the time he was drafted, he had not made up his mind.

When he saw me, he came up the steps more rapidly and with a smile on his face. His glasses had slipped halfway down his nose, so that he had to lift his head to look at me. I thought he was going to hug me, but then, at the last moment, he stuck out his arm to shake my hand. There was affection in his eyes but not in his family tradition. He once described them as a very proper American family with pioneer roots in Ohio. When I first met them I was very impressed. They looked like a family made in Hollywood for an old movie about good, God-fearing people. The gray-haired professor, the smiling and corseted wife, and the daughter waiting for a Harvard man to come courting.

"My goodness, look at you," he said. "You've grown a lot since I last saw you."

"I guess so," I said, pleased that he noticed. I was wearing a hand-me-down tweed jacket from a cousin in Florida. My grandmother still sent us packages to help out, even though my father had died eleven years earlier. My

218

mother patched and sewed and ironed to get the most out of my shirts and socks and underweear.

"You were just a boy when I left," he said. "Now you're a handsome young man about to graduate from high school."

I didn't know what to say next, so I shrugged, as if to indicate that time and nature deserved the compliment, not me. Then I just changed the subject to keep from blushing. "Can you tell me what you did in the war?" I said. "Or is it still a secret?"

We were walking towards a restaurant not far from the library, a Spanish place with posters of bullfighting on the walls. "It's all right now to talk about the war, but not my next assignment," he said. "I'm being sent to a base in South Dakota. In England I was part of the ground crew. I had to keep track of the planes that returned, in order to estimate our losses.The Air Force didn't like the enemy to know how tough it was."

"Was it real bad?" I said.

We came to the restaurant, a simple-looking place. He didn't answer until we were inside. There were clusters of garlic hanging from the arch that led to the kitchen, and there was the sound of recorded guitar music, distant, as if from another room, and by a man who was sad or in love.

"Yes," he said. "It was very bad. We had to wait and wait, after the big raids, to see who came back and who was missing. They were mostly B-17s with crews of ten men. If they did not get back to the base, there was still a chance that they would show up somewhere, or were ditched in the sea. When all the reports were filed, we had to list the dead and those who were just missing in action. It was a nasty job. I knew a lot of the men who were lost."

"What are the ribbons for?" I said. "Did you get any medals?"

"No, just routine overseas service."

"But it was an important job," I said. "They should have made you an officer."

"They offered me a commission, but I turned it down," he said.

"How come?"

"I just wanted to do my duty, nothing more. I didn't want any authority, and I didn't want to get deeply involved. I don't believe in war, but in this case what could we do? Hitler has to be defeated. His dreams of world conquest and racial purification are insane. Those concentration camps are human slaughterhouses. It's all coming out now."

"Do you think it will be over soon?" I said.

"In Europe maybe. The Allies have moved very rapidly. Some of our troops have crossed the German border. And the Russians are moving steadily into eastern Europe. They'd like to get to Berlin before us. And if General Patton had his way, he wouldn't stop until he reached Moscow. General Eisenhower ought to relieve him of his command for saying things like that."

"Did you see any of those buzz-bombs or rockets?" I said.

"I heard them, but I didn't always see them," he said. "They passed over us on their was to London. One came down on the base. It's really frightening. You hear the rocket engine, and then all of a sudden it cuts out and you don't hear anything. That's the most frightening part of it, because as soon as the engine cuts out you know it's coming down somewhere with a ton of explosives. I saw one in London. Devastating! It must have leveled five buildings and killed a hundred people."

I tried to imagine the scene, the sound of the jet engine in the night sky, the eerie silence, then the enormous explosion, buildings collapsing and on fire, people screaming, dying, being blown apart, their arms and legs broken off, their faces torn to piece, blood on white plaster walls, like abstract art. I found it hard to believe that he had seen these things. I looked at him in his neat uniform, his tie and buttons, his glasses. And then I thought of all those poor crew members, shot to pieces, sometimes with a full bomb load on board, evaporated in a cloud of destruction, spiraling earthward, sucked into the sea.

Suddenly, a waiter was standing beside our table, a pencil in his hand, a smile on his face. "I'll have the *gazpacho* and special salad," said Mr. Alexander. Most of the menu was meaningless to me. I ordered an omelet and potatoes.

The interruption allowed us to get away from the war and talk about something else. I knew that sooner or later he would ask me about college applications. "I talked to Mrs. Applebaum, the college advisor at my school," I said. "My friends and I call her Mrs. Appletree. She said that my grades are not good enough for the Arista Society and that she would recommend City College. I told her that my average was 88% and that I had a varsity letter in track. She said I was being impudent. And she reminded me that I would need a recommendation from James Monroe High School in order to get into college."

The waiter put a large salad on the table that was alive with olives and lettuce, tomatoes and green peppers, sliced eggs and artichoke hearts. We both stared at it for a moment, as though it was not quite relevant yet.

"Would you like to try for Columbia?" he said.

I felt a flutter of excitement, but my reply was almost a whisper. I fixed my eyes on the white tablecloth. "I've dreamt about it for years. Do you really think I might have a chance?"

"I'll have to talk to Dean Carmen. He and my father have been close friends for many years. Maybe there's a scholarship for someone like you. Talented but poor."

"That's me," I said, "and I can run like the wind."

We laughed, and then I got serious again. "What about Mrs. Appletree?"

"Don't worry," he said. "Columbia is not bound by the policies of your high school. They like to have students from all forty-eight states and as many foreign countries as possible, and different economic circumstances. They don't admit many New Yorkers."

"Why not?"

"Because they get a lot of applications, and--"

"And what?" I said.

"And because a lot of the good students are Jewish. Don't get me wrong; it's not prejudice. If a lot of Irish students from Boston applied, it would be the same problem. It's broad representation they want."

Our food came. We ate and talked. "Are you still interested in being a doctor?" he said.

I told him I wasn't sure, but I would probably put that on my application, because I couldn't think of anything else. "My English teacher thinks I'm a brilliant writer, but what's the point of studying something you already know how to do?"

He told me what an English major was expected to

222

do, and it sounded hard. A huge amount of reading and some foreign languages. "I'm not taking anymore French," I said. "It ruined my average and kept me out of the Arista Society. And I still can't speak it or read it."

25

Down By The River

The unlikely romance between me and Jeanne Emmanuel was threatening to settle into something permanent. Our familiarity was untainted by contempt, and we were compatible when it came to ideas. Neither of us was willing to take the giant step forward into the dark world of sexual intercourse, having been warned in a euphemism-filled lecture on "social behavior," meaning Sex Education, that, if we had sex, we risked disease, death, criminal prosecution, pregnancy, heartbreak, poverty, and insanity.

We whispered and giggled over the lecture because it was so juvenile and puritanical. We felt like an intelligent and committed couple, even though we were young and inexperienced. We loved our sensual explorations, but we knew how babies were conceived and were careful not to go too far. Jeanne was hardly a voluptuous woman. Her body was still developing, still a bit childlike. Her breasts were small and her nipples unused. She was still learning how to feel things in certain parts of her body, but we did not have the luxury of a place where we could take off all our clothes. In school it was nice to hug our secret, the little intimacies that bound us together and made us feel special and grown up. We had agreed not to tell anyone and we kept our promises.

Jeanne had very dark hair, in which she started wearing a flower to go with her smile. Her friends might

224

have suspected something, but she was an unlikely looking suspect. She dressed plainly and wore no makeup. There was nothing at all seductive in her manner or speech. What was attractive about her was her mind, her quickness, her quiet humor, and the light in her eyes. We felt we knew each other very well, though neither of us knew much about the other's home life. At first this did not seem to matter very much, since ours was a school romance, the sort of thing that runs its course. Occasionally, it continues into engagement and marriage, but, in our case, that was going to be almost impossible, given the strong feelings of her Jewish parents.

As my senior year wore on, we began to talk about my graduation. She wanted to know where I would go to college and how I would feel about her. Would I go out with other girls? College girls? I reassured her. I said that she was my girlfriend and that I would be loyal to her. Things like that usually brought some color back into her pale cheeks. And sometimes, now, she began to shed some quiet tears. I never had to deal with a girl who cried and I found it disturbing. The only way I could respond was to comfort her, even if it required an occasional lie. I actually had no idea what would become of our romance, and I secretly looked forward to meeting some college girls, but I was pretty sure that I loved Jeanne, even though I had fantasies that might upset her.

Pretty soon I learned that women mature, emotionally, more quickly than men. And they start planning their future in an incredibly detailed way. I was still a boy from East Harlem, trying to run faster than the wind around a real cinder track. I needed love desperately, because I was about to leave home and face the world alone. Once I was out of the house, I knew I would not want to come back, or even look back. It would be like crouching down in the starting blocks at a track meet. As soon as the gun was fired, I'd be out of there. I think I knew, halfway through my senior year that our love affair was doomed to end. Where, when, or how I didn't know. I said that we would go on seeing each other, but I knew it would be difficult, no matter what college I went to. She believed me because she wanted it to be that way. She would even be willing to break with her family, she said, even though that might kill her father, who had a bad heart. My thinking stumbled at that point and I usually said something cheerful like, "Let's go for a walk by the river." I meant the Bronx River, a polluted stream that ran through some marshland not far from the high school. It was not as nice as Pelham Park, but it was green and often private enough for a warm embrace in the cold months. Most of the people who did walk there were just walking their dog.

Sometimes we would go there with Weinberg, the only old friend of mine who I still saw regularly. Lesko had to drop out of school entirely for reasons that he kept secret. He had moved out of his parents' apartment and was staying with his sister in a nice neighborhood downtown. She was actually his half-sister, since his mother had been married twice. By our senior year Weinberg was showing some signs of growing up. He had gotten a bit taller and thinner, and he was definitely going to college. His parents would help him. For some reason I did not make many new friends at James Monroe High School. I got along with some students, some of Mamie Wallach's favorites, but I never went to their homes. I was more inclined to go home on the subway and to take part in some of the social activities at the church. I also had a busy imagination and did not mind spending time alone. Later on, I would be able to say that all I really needed was a typewriter and a female companion to get by in life.

Mr. Alexander wasn't able to find out anything further about Columbia before he was transferred to an Army Air Force Base in Rapid City, South Dakota, where the B-29 super bombers were stationed. He didn't know whether or not he would be assigned to the Pacific. He said he hadn't heard anything from his father, who was very busy in Washington,D.C.

It was Christmas time, and at home we were all on edge, because we knew that our days on 112th Street were limited. The threat of change was making my mother nervous. The building was deteriorating physically. The janitor and his family had moved out a long time ago, and he was replaced by the alcoholic who lived in the basement and screamed in the night from bad dreams. He took care of the furnace and sometimes mopped the halls. The owner warned us that he was probably going to abandon the building to the City soon because his company could no longer pay the taxes or upkeep. Several apartments were already boarded up to keep out poachers and burglars. We heard that an unlicensed dentist was moving into the apartment below ours. And two women took another apartment and went into business. Whatever business they did was conducted in Spanish and accompanied by loud music most of the night.

But some signs of the old order still persisted. The iceman still delivered blocks of ice, lugging them up the stairs in a butter bucket that he carried on his shoulder, which was padded with a wet rag. He, too, was talking about quitting this block and moving east to Second Avenue. The Kruglers would last another few months, leaving mostly strangers, some of whom could not speak any English. If it wasn't for the church people, we would probably have moved a lot sooner. We managed to keep a little civilized community going, and we still celebrated the holidays of Christmas and Easter. The congregation now included several respectable Puerto Rican families, who dressed up, as we all did, for the Sunday service.

One day, my mother told us that her old aunt, who lived on 105th Steet between Third Avenue and Second Avenue, was urging her to move there, because the block was still Italian and because there might be an apartment available soon.

She announced this to us as though it were bad news. Aunt Maria was her mother's sister. She was so fat that she could not leave her apartment. She had a stepdaughter who brought her homework from a local sweat shop. All she did all day was to sew and crochet and complain about the injustices of her past. She had been mistreated, neglected, betrayed and widowed. But there she was in perpetual black, still knitting and sewing and cursing those who ruined her life. My mother told her that she would think about the apartment if it became available. It did, and she thought about it until it was taken by someone else. After that, she thought it might be a good idea to move to 105th Street when something else became available.

Meanwhile, life went on. Every school day I caught the subway at 110th Street and rode up to the Bronx. Jeanne and I talked and walked and tried not to think about the future. I tried to call her on weekends, but sometimes I got her father on the phone and had to hang up. We still did not have a phone at home.

I got letters from Mr. Alexander about how cold it was in South Dakota, and about how busy his father was ever since he beccame a government economic advisor. I began to wonder whether or not he would remember to talk to Dean Carmen. And I worried also about the possibility that Mr. Alexander might be sent to the Pacific.

In the early spring of 1945, time seemed to be slipping away more quickly. Roosevelt was reelected for a fourth term in November and inaugurated in January. In his newspaper pictures he looked frail and old, worn down by the war and his partial paralysis. He usually appeared riding in a car or standing at a podium, where he had to be placed by his sons. More often now he faced the camera from a chair or from behind a desk. The press was discreet enough to avoid any discussion of his health.

One day, Jeanne and I decided to go for a walk by the Bronx River. Weinberg (Jeanne called him Sidney) tagged along, since we would soon be taking the subway home together. We talked about the war in Europe, which seemed to be coming to a violent end with Hitler prepared to fight to the death and proving it in the Battle of the Bulge, a massive counterattack that took the Allies by surprise.

It was a mild, sunny day, and even the murky Bronx River looked pleasant, though the grassy banks along the dirt path were marred by litter. It was not far to the elevated subway and a rim of dreary apartment houses.

We talked about summer jobs. Weinberg said he was going to work with his father in the market. I said I'd like to get a job in the Public Library. And Jeanne said her father didn't want her to work yet, even though she had just turned sixteen. Jeanne and I were hoping to find jobs close to one another.

"Her father doesn't trust her," I said.

"He knows I've been seeing you," said Jeanne, "even though I deny it. He says you call and then hang up."

"Maybe I should speak to him next time, just to prove that I am a worthwhile human being and no threat to his daughter's spiritual life.'

"Maybe if I promise to marry a Jew, he'll let you be my friend for a while."

"*I'll* marry you," said Weinberg. "I'm a Jew. I go to Hebrew school, I'm circumcised. What more do you want? You can even see this jerk once in a while." He turned to me, "But it'll cost you. Nothing for nothing!"

We were still laughing when we sat down on the stone bench. A stray dog came by sniffing the ground, and then two young men in overalls appeared. I had lived so long in East Harlem that I could feel when something was not right. They were talking to each other and looking in our direction. Were they talking about us?

When they got closer I could see that one was about sixteen and the other was closer to twenty. He was also broader and taller. His hair was uncombed and he looked as though he might have been doing construction work. He put a cigarette in his lips and then patted his pockets, as if he was out of matches. I knew he would stop by us.

"Hey, you got a match?" he said to me.

"I don't smoke," I said.

"How about you, Fatso?" he said to Weinberg, who turned speechless and pale. His glance lingered on Jeanne for a long moment. "Is she your girlfriend?" he said to me.

.   I knew it would be a mistake to let him know that I was afraid. I ignored his question and said to Jeanne and Weinberg, "Let's go. It's getting late." I took her hand and led her a few steps towards the populated streets in the distance. Her hand was cold.

"Wait a minute," he said. "You haven't answered my question." His voice was angry, as though we had done something to offend him. His younger friend touched his arm, as if to calm him down, and then he looked at us apologetically. I was relieved to see at least one of them was sane. But then the rough one pulled away from his friend. "Who the fuck does he think he is? I haven't done anything to him. Not yet, anyway." He walked closer to me and repeated his question. "I said is she your girlfriend?" His tone was menacing, and I could see in his eyes that he was dangerous, perhaps insane or on drugs. He looked at Jeanne. "Do you think she'll dance for me? How old is she?"

"Fifteen," said Jeanne in a trembling whisper. It was a lie. I knew what she was trying to do.

For an endless moment the scene was frozen: the hazy sun over the murky river, the rim of apartment houses too far away. Weinberg paralyzed by fear. Jeanne standing almost behind me, still holding my hand. Suddenly, I reached into the pocket of my corduroy jacket, as if I had a weapon there. I grabbed a fountain pen and pushed it foreward. He stepped away, and, in the same motion, he put his hand down the front of his overalls and drew out a long kitchen knife. "Oh yeah!" he shouted. "What do you got? What do you got? A knife? I'll show you a knife, pretty boy. I'll show it to your girlfriend too."

My heart thumped, my face flushed. From the

231

corner of my eye I could see Weinberg break into a run.
Both guys looked confused. "Never mind him," said the
one with the knife. "And you!" He jabbed the knife in my
direction."Let me see what you got in that pocket."

"Nothing!" I said.

"He ain't got nothing," the friend said.

"Turn your pocket out, so I can see."

I pulled the pocket out and showed him the
fountain pen. He laughed. "What a fucking idiot you are.
You could get killed doing something like that. Isn't that
right, Leon?"

"Yeah! Don't make him mad," said Leon to me.

I could see that he wanted to leave. He whispered
to the crazy one, "Maybe the fat guy is calling a cop. We
better get out of here."

"Shut up, Leon. You're scaring the girl. Look at
her."

Jeanne was pale, even too frightened to cry.

"She's only fifteen," said Leon.

"Don't worry about it." He came close to Jeanne
and told me to move away. I hesitated. He pushed the knife
at me, and I was convinced that he would use it. I had to
back off and find some kind of weapon.

He gave Jeanne a thin-lipped wet smile. "Don't be
scared, honey. I just want to see what you're wearing
under that dress. He tried to lift it with the point of the
knife. She was too frightened to run or even to hold down
her skirt. He lifted it high enough to see her underwear. It
was a childish cotton garment.

"She's just a kid," said Leon.

"Oh yeah? We'll see."

I was frantic. I had to do something in a hurry. I

232

backed further away, and, while they were not looking, I picked up a hefty rock. Throwing it would not be good enough. I had to rush him and smash him in the head. I heard myself screaming like some kind of savage warrior. Both men were startled. I crossed the line into blind rage. It was me or them. I charged, my hand holding the rock. I aimed for his face and he looked suddenly confused. He raised the knife, as if to ward off the blow. The knife hit the rock and fell, but at the same time he swung at me with his other hand, a clenched fist. He hit me in the eye. My blow missed his face. I was still screaming. I imagined tearing out his throat with my bare hands. I bent down to pick up another stone. Leon picked up the knife and shouted, "Let's get out of here. That guy's gone crazy." They backed off and then broke into a run towards some trees.

Jeanne and I walked back. We saw no sign of Weinberg or the police. We assumed that he just caught the subway and went home. I was amazed at what had happened, and shocked at my own reactions. I rode with Jeanne to her station, and then I kissed her and said, "You'll be all right. I'll see you tomorrow."

"Let's not tell anybody," she said. "Do you mind?"

"Of course not. Your family would be very upset."

"They would report it to the police."

"Don't worry. Try to forget it," I said. On my way home I kept going over and over the incident, until I was convinced that there was nothing else I could have done.

233

26

The Passionate Spaniard

Coming of age is difficult enough, but when you add financial and family problems and a violent neighborhood that is declining into chaos, then you really have trouble. My friends and I all wanted to get out of East Harlem, but it was easier said than done. We all wanted to feel grown up, and we all were interested in girls, but had very little experience. None of us felt like men. We had no accomplishments, no money, no visible proof that we were men and not boys. We did not want to prove ourselves in street fights. It was dangerous and pointless. Besides, we were all afraid, or at least cautious. One guy against a gang was frightening. At times, we all felt like failures. Lesko had proven himself against Alvarez, but he did not want to go on doing that kind of thing. Neither did I, after standing my ground against Jeanne's attacker. And neither did Quintero, after a few scuffles. Weinberg was the only one who was not embarrassed by running away from danger, even if it meant abandoning his friends and his self-respect. "I don't care," he once said. "Nothing matters but staying alive. Once you're dead you can't even be a hero." Because we lived in the shadow of the war, one of our favorite subjects for debate was: "Would you rather be a dead hero or a live coward?"

Quintero was the most romantic member of our gang and the one who was most out of touch with reality. He had to deal with being an immigrant from Cuba, with a

234

family that was very Catholic, and with a father who was severe, especially with his daughter. He had artistic talent, but he didn't know what to do with it. Recognition in school was not enough, and his family was not sympathetic. They thought he should get a job and make some money like everybody else. Eventually, he began to develop illusions of grandeur. He called himself "The Passionate Spaniard," but he was hopelessly awkward with women. He read *Don Quixote* and identified with him. He took up bodybuilding and looked tall and muscular, but he could not get rid of his expresion of distaste, even disgust, at times. He cultivated "the El Greco look."

During my senior year at Monroe, he fell in love with my sister, who simply laughed at him. When he persisted and confessed his desire to make love to her and marry her, she got angry and frightened. He felt her rejection as a great humiliation, but he kept sticking his hand in the fire and making his hurt feelings known to all of us. Eventually, his obsession led to an unpleasant incident.

He dropped out of school for a while and found some menial work from time to time. He did not give up his art, but he did mostly sketches of his friends or models in a workshop. He had not lost his sense of humor, but it became more and more about sex. He revealed, half humorously, his techniques for masturbation. "Look at yourself in the mirror," he said one day. We knew he was slipping into a strange state of mind, but we did not know how serious it was. My sister was very outspoken about how he followed her around. She was going to the High School of Commerce and studying to be a secretary. He would wait for her outside of school and come home with her. He claimed that he was protecting her, because we

235

lived in a bad neighborhood and he had heard the Puerto Rican boys saying dirty things about her. He said they made him very angry, but he never did anything to them. He just went on following my sister and talking to her romantically. She didn't know what to do about it.

My mother the survivor said, "If you had a steady boyfriend, you would get rid of him in a hurry, but, as long as he doesn't do anything violent, you can just ignore him. Having him around might make you safer in this neighborhood. He speaks Spanish. They might think he's one of them." My mother's view of men was that they all wanted sex, and that women had to take care of themselves until some nice guy came along and said, "Put on a white dress, we're getting married." And then she told us for the thousandth time how she and my father got married. "He didn't ask me; he told me," she said with a girlish laugh. "What did I know about such things?"

My sister had a part-time job in an office downtown. Perhaps it was part of her training. Quintero began to show up outside the apartment building in the morning, so that he could "escort" her. And then he would be waiting again when she got out. Sometimes he called her at work, which made her very angry. And he went on writing love letters to her, which occasionally she showed us, as if they were laughable. He was a very eccentric figure, comic and sad. But he was still part of the gang, though we were not exactly kind and understanding. We teased him and mocked him with his own tag, *The Passionate Spaniard.*

One day, my sister warned him not to follow her downtown, but he did anyway. Perhaps she was planning to meet someone else there, and wanted to avoid trouble.

236

When they arrived at the office building, their argument grew more heated, and he became more stubborn. Finally, she threatened to call the police if he didn't leave her alone. He didn't believe her, and the argument went on and grew louder. A cop noticed the disturbance and came over to ask, "What's the trouble here? Is everything all right? Do you know this guy? Is he bothering you?" My sister was afraid to say anything at first. She had to admit she knew him, but she finally said that he was following her around and that he wouldn't go away and leave her alone. That's all the cop had to hear. He told Quintero to stop annoying her and to move on, but Quintero refused and said something abusive that made the cop angry. He tried to take Quintero by the arm to urge him to get going, but Quintero thought he was being arrested and pulled away. There was a scuffle that got rough and the cop had to subdue Quintero and call for assistance from a police box. Since they were New York City cops, they were familiar with unbalanced people. They had a whole routine for handling them. Usually they wound up in Bellevue Hospital's psychiatric ward and were held there for observation. They got my sister to file a complaint.

Later, when she told us all about it she was trembling and upset. "I didn't want to get him into trouble, but he really scares me. He needs help." In her own way, she was being apologetic to me and his other friends. We didn't blame her for anything, but there was an old loyalty to the group and hostility to the police that made her feel that she had betrayed the gang. This feeling was especially strong in Italian neighborhoods

When we heard that Quintero was being held at Bellevue for observation, we were all a bit shook up. We knew he was strange, but we never really wrestled with the idea of insanity. Maybe because we all felt a little crazy in that changing neighborhood. Of course, we went to see him, but not without an argument from Weinberg, who didn't think we were obliged to do so. "I don't think he would come to see me if I was in Bellevue," he said.

"Neither would I," said Lesko.

"Sure you would," I said.

He was caught off guard. We were not sentimental about such things, but we had gone through school together as kids, all those years. It wasn't exactly us against the world, but we were glad we all went to see Quintero after we finished arguing the point in philosophical terms.

Bellevue Hospital was a dreary place, especially the ward for alcoholics and the mentally disturbed. I had been there once with my mother, just before my father died. The yellow walls and green linoleum brought it all back. Twelve years passed in a moment, and there we were, walking down the same hall. We were alone and sixteen years old and not used to the smell of death. We had come to see our friend who had lost his way. Suddenly, we were all children again.

We were led into a large visiting area, where a lot of people, mostly men, shuffled around in pale-green, wrinkled bathrobes. Most of them did not have visitors. Their movements seemed aimless and random. Some sat staring at the floor, as if the secret code to sanity was to be found in the dark tiles. There were few conversations going on, but the place was unbelievably noisy. Where was it coming from? It sounded like static.

A nurse with a starched cap showed us which of these lost souls was Quintero. In spite of the sad setting, he wore the same small smile that he had developed in his decline into confusion. It gave him the look of one who had been betrayed. He looked at us. We looked at him. At first we didn't know what to expect. We had heard about shock treatments and straight jackets, but we had never been to a place like this. Then he spoke and he sounded the same as always. "Welcome to Bellevue," he said. "Isn't this stupid? What am I doing in a place like this? I'm not crazy, you know. Just in love. Is there a law against that?"

"So what's going to happen here?" said Weinberg.

"They are going to observe me," said Qintero, with that odd smile. "I don't know what they expect to find."

'We heard that you hit a cop," said Lesko.

"Who told you that?"

"His sister," he said, nodding at me. "She said you wouldn't stop following her."

"Is there a law against that?" said Quintero.

"I don't know," said Lesko, "I'm not a lawyer, but if you were bothering her, I guess she had a right to protect herself."

"Against what?"

"Against you," said Weinberg.

"Me? She didn't need to be protected from me. I would never hurt her. I love her. *The Passionate Spaniard* loves her. I never thought she would do this to me."

They stood by a barred window. Backlighted, he looked like the El Greco figure he always wanted to be. His frown was deeper. His eyes were darker. He began to look a bit confused.

"So what's going to happen now?" I said.

"They can't keep me here. I'll take some tests and then they'll have to let me go."

239

"What kind of tests?" I said.

"I don't know. Crazy tests, I guess, like two plus two is five." We all laughed. At that moment he did, in fact, seem sane.

"Why did you hit the cop?" said Weinberg. "You can get into deep shit hitting a cop."

"I didn't hit him, but I did resist him. Love makes you do strange things. But now that she has betrayed me, I may have to give her up. Anyhow, I'm seventeen now and pretty soon I'll be eighteen and in the army. I'll probably get killed in the Pacific somewhere."

"Why don't you flunk one of your tests and get a deferment?" said Weinberg, who dreaded the possibility of being drafted.

"And why don't you go fuck yourself, you fat coward?" said Quintero, and then looked around as though he was overheard by an attendant. He forced himself to whisper. "If I wasn't crazy when I came in, I might get crazy from being here. You don't know how much it means to me that you guys came." A rim of tears formed in his eyes.

We changed the subject. He told us about Pilgrim State Hospital on Long Island. "After I'm observed, I might be sent out there," he said. "It's like being in a zoo here. Remember the good times we had in the zoo? Remember the monkeys jerking off and the people laughing at them?"

When it was time for us to leave, he looked a little frantic, as if we were his only hope. But what could we do, except visit him now and then?

240

27

Nightmare Days

There was chaos in Europe as the Third Reich collapsed into ruins and the horror stories and nightmares emerged from the liberated concentration camps. There were heaps of dead bodies at Buchenwald, where fifty thousand Jews had been murdered and twenty thousand barely survived, almost skeletons, too weak to understand what was happening.

Nothing in the whole war was more horrible than these mass killings, but at the same time something happened at home that shocked America and made us weep. President Franklin D. Roosevelt died suddenly of a cerebral hemorrhage at his cottage in Warm Springs, Georgia. He was our leader, the only president many of us ever knew. He saw us through the Great Depression and a World War that was about to end in an Allied victory. I was four years old when he was first elected.

The day this happened, April 12, 1945, the history club of James Monroe High School was scheduled to take part in a radio program on Latin American problems. We had done our homework. I had written a script. Mamie rehearsed us. We were all excited about being on the radio that evening. On the afternoon of April 12th, we were suddenly told that the radio program had been cancelled. We were not told why. I did not find out until I arrived home.

As I rode the subway, I had a strange feeling, one of

those premonitions that can not be explained. Somehow I knew that the President had died. I ran home from the station and turned on the radio. The news had just been announced at 5:48 PM. I was on the subway at the time. How could I have known?

Everything seemed to be falling apart. Cities were being reduced to rubble by our bombers in Europe and in the Pacific. The Russians closed in from the east and the Allies from the west.

In East Harlem there was another kind of war zone. Our landlord abandoned our building. The city then condemned it and ordered everyone to move out by a certain date. One by one, the apartments were boarded up. Garbage accumulated in the hallways, and some of the lights went out but were not replaced. Lesko's family moved further east on 115th Street, close to the wire factory where his father worked. Weinberg's family also moved somewhere safer, but continued to work in the market. Without the constant company of my old gang, life got more dangerous for me. Coming and going I had to look both ways from the stoop to see if there were any Puerto Rican guys hanging around. They did not always bother me, especially if I moved briskly and got to the subway station or back home. At times, they moved in my direction and I just took off and ran home. One day, they saw me coming up from the subway station at 110th. I had to go two blocks. They taunted me, as usual. "You got a nickel, Americano? You got money?" I knew what was coming, so I just ran, but this time one of them followed me into the hallway and all the way up to the third floor, also running. I got into the apartment. No one was home. I locked the door and caught my breath. In another moment there was a banging at the door.The hair stood up on the back of my neck. Then I heard the rough voice of a man. "Police! Open up!"

I opened the door cautiously. I saw the uniform and felt safer. He had the kid by the arm. He asked me some questions. I told him that my mother lived here and my father was dead. You're Italian, right?" I nodded."I took a knife off this kid," said the cop. "Do you want me to take him in? What do you want me to do to him? Anything you say."

I looked at the boy. He looked at me. I knew there would be more trouble if I filed a complaint. "No," I said. "Just tell him to leave me alone. We'll be moving out of here soon."

The cop shrugged. "OK!" Then he turned to the boy and stuck his night stick into his lean stomach. "Do you understand English?'

The kid nodded."

"You leave this boy, alone. *Comprende?* The next time, we send you to jail, you fucking scumbag." He shoved the kid into the hallway and we heard him scampering down the stairs. "Jesus!" he said to me, "What's a nice family doing in this fucking dump? Tell your mother to get out of here before they tear the building down on all of you. If you need help finding an apartment, see Marc. You know, Marcantonio, 116th St. Everybody knows where his office is. The door is open. Now just be careful, kid. All right?"

His Italian-American accent was unmistakable. It was a pleasure to hear it again. I remembered my grandmother, who came to stay with us after my father died. She hardly spoke English at all. And I remembered the uncles and aunts and cousins in my mother's family. I couldn't wait until we moved further east, back into the Italian neighborhood.

From our windows we could look down into the rubble in the back yards, which looked like battlefields where a war had killed off all the vegetation. The big tree in the yard next door was a corpse of a tree that once flourished in a patch of grass. The soil was no longer visible. It was down there somewhere under about three feet of garbage. Rats came out at night to look it over, and tough alley cats stalked them. Between poles and tenement houses, clotheslines were strung like heavy threads in spider webs.

Jungle sounds filled the night. Laughing hyenas and howling cats. The throb of Puerto Rican music. Voices from open windows without curtains. The rituals of primitive tribes, New York style. In its death throes, the building reminded me of those pictures in the newspapers of cities like Dresden, which was reduced to rubble by massive Allied bombing just two months earlier. In a letter, Mr. Alexander said it was totally unnecessary, since the war was almost over and Dresden had been spared until then as a city of art and culture. About a hundred thousand people were killed in those raids. Hardly anything was left standing. Our building on 112th Street was like this on a much smaller scale. There was no heat, no hot water. Vandals thumped across the roof and pissed in the hallways. My mother was finally moved by utter necessity. She went back to her aunt, who spoke to some friends, and found a vacant apartment in the building next to her. However, it was the top floor, a five-story walk-up. "We'll never get the iceman to bring up the ice," said my mother. But my brother and sister and I were so relieved to be getting out, that we would have taken anything.

28

Everything Ends and Begins

As the war moved towards its conclusion, we all wondered what the post-war world would be like. It was, after all, a world war, and, therefore, the whole world would be changed. That was the impression we all had. An end of violence and death, men marching home, shining cities rising from the rubble. Peace and Justice and Prosperity. I remembered our visit to the World's Fair of 1939. We were still kids, still naive enough to believe in Futurama, the General Motors view of things to come. Now it suddenly seemed to me like just new cars and highways and high-rise buildings. Wasn't there more to it than that?

Shortly after Roosevelt's death on April 12th, Mussolini, the Italian dictator, was executed by an angry mob and his body hanged upside down alongside the body of his mistress and two other Fascists. Two days later, on April 30th, Adolf Hitler committed suicide in a bunker with his long-time mistress Eva Braun, whom he married just before his death. Within days, the Russian army was in control of Berlin and had linked up with the Americans to cut Germany in two. Some of the soldiers who resisted were teen-age boys, some of them wearing uniforms too large for them. Everything moved very quickly. Victory was not a simple thing. It was a chaos of tragedy and triumph. Some would live, some would die, but everyone wanted it to be over.

On May 7th, the Germans surrendered, and a great spontaneous victory celebration took place in Times Square. There was no plan. It just seemed the natural thing to do. It was the heart of the city, which was the heart of the country, and the center of the universe as far as we were concerned. A rim of headlines in lights moved around The New York Times Building. Letter by letter it spelled out the end of the war in Europe. UNCONDITIONAL SURRENDER OF GERMANY. DOCUMENT SIGNED IN REIMS. NAZI TROOPS LAY DOWN THEIR ARMS ON ALL FRONTS.

New York came alive, like a river running down to the sea in a flood. My friends and I managed to get some quarts of beer and hitch a ride south. Before long all the avenues leading to Times Square were jammed. We were on the outside of cars and trucks and trolleys, hanging by one hand, waving our bottles in the other, shaking them so that they sprayed on others and on our own faces. Everyone was laughing, shouting, and singing. At sixteen, my friends and I had not yet learned how to drink, but this was a special occasion and we wanted to be part of it.

When the traffic finally stopped completely, we jumped off the running board of an old Buick and continued on foot. The crowd thickened as we got closer to Times Square. There were many men in uniforms and many women in spring dresses and ribbons and bright red lipstick. Sometimes they glanced at us, as if they wondered why we too were not in uniforms. But the war in Europe was over now and nobody seemed to care about anything but that, even if the Japanese were still undefeated in the Pacific.

It seemed impossible to get any closer to Times

Square than a few blocks, but we kept pushing through the mass of people, feeling the warmth of their bodies, looking into the faces and eyes of strangers, who now looked like members of one large family. Women kissed the military men, as if to thank them for winning the war. And the men responded as though these women were their reward for landing in Normandy or flying through enemy flak to bomb the oilfields of Rumania, or simply for patrolling the coast of New Jersey. We wished we were a little older or in uniforms, but we got our share of being pressed together with the bodies of woman. We even got a random kiss now and again from teen-age girls, who took advantage of the orgiastic celebration to try out their lips and limbs. Everybody was having fun, including the pickpockets. I saw one at work but turned away, remembering the stolen money that lost me my job at the pharmacy.

Church bells clanged, sirens wailed. There were even some trumpets in the crowd blaring out the cavalry charge. It was a day for all of us to remember, but mainly those who fought the war and those who waited, sometimes in vain, for their loved ones to return.

Among the other things that ended for me was high school. In June, I graduated, and was glad, because it meant I could move on to more important things in life. But before I graduated I had to deal with the disapproval of the staff at James Monroe.

I had finally gotten to see Dean Carmen at Columbia, through Mr. Alexander, of course. And it was a very pleasant meeting. He was a kindly elderly man in his last years at the college. He had been told my story in brief, but asked me to go over it again. I did not try to exaggerate the difficulties of growing up poor in East Harlem without a father. He listened carefully, his pale blue eyes fixed on me. He seemed especially interested in the fact that my father had been in the U.S. Navy. He asked me about my interests. I told him that I wanted to be a doctor, but was also interested in writing and philosophy, and psychology. As I went on adding subjects, he smiled and said, "You'll have time to think about such things, after the basic courses in Humanities and Contemporary Civilization." He hesitated. "Providing we can find a place for you here, of course."

I felt comfortable with him, and left full of encouragement. A few days later I went to see Rev. Wilson, who also went to Columbia and had good connections there. He was pleased that I had applied and said he would do what he could to help. He talked about a summer job on the campus, if I was admitted. He knew the Admissions Director, it turned out, which proved to be an advantage.

At James Monroe, I was called into the Principal's Office to meet with him, his assistant and Miss Applebaum, my advisor. They wanted to discuss this advantage. The principal was annoyed that I had applied to Columbia in spite of the fact that I was told not to. I could speak more boldly now that I had been encouraged by Dean Carmen and Rev. Wilson. "I was advised to apply directly by one of the faculty members," I said.

"And how did you come to know a faculty member?" said Miss Applebaum.

"I knew his son, who was a volunteer at the Boys Club of New York. Mr. Alexander has been giving me advice since I was eleven years old."

"But we warned you here that we might not be able to support your application to Columbia," she said.

I paused to find the right words. "Mr. Alexander thought you were wrong about that. He said I had a perfect right to file an application to any college I wanted to, and he thought it was peculiar of you to try to keep me from applying to Columbia, since I've been a very good student here and just missed being an Arista student by two percentage points, mainly because I had a poor grade in French. Mr. Alexander thought I should have been advised to take Spanish."

The Principal cleared his throat and asked me to wait outside for a minute. The minute turned into fifteen minutes. I sat on a bench and watched the girls go by.

When I was called back into the office, it was the Principal who talked to me. The others listend with serious expressions on their faces. "Now that you have made your application, there is nothing we can do about it, except to wish you well," he said. "Naturally, James Monroe will be proud of anyone who can get into an Ivy League college."

Nobody said anything else. The conference was over and we all went our separate ways. We did not get into the New York or ethnic prejudice. About two weeks later, I was sent a letter of acceptance by Dean Carmen.

Shortly after I informed Rev. Wilson, he told me that there would be a summer job for me in the Admissions Office. The Director, Mr. Ireland, was an old friend of his.

I was given a scholarship that was intended for a deserving student whose father or grandfather had served in the U.S. Navy. It was one of many scholarships with special conditions or in memory of certain alumni.

I was afraid to get too excited at first, because

something might go wrong and it would prove to be a mistake. When I was sure that I was in, I got on the Third Avenue trolley, which went up to 125th Street and turned west to go across town, right through Harlem to Amsterdam Avenue, where I could transfer and get a Broadway trolley to the Columbia campus, which was on Morningside Heights. From there I could look back over the dark rooftops of Harlem all the way to the East River. I stood at the railing for a long time and thought about all the things that were ending now.

I would never go to Wilson's summer camp again. I would never see Ida Moon. I would never have to live at home after the summer. And that would be spent in the apartment on 105th Street. The old building would be torn down, along with six square blocks of other buildings to make way for the James Weldon Johnson housing development. I would never go to the Boys Club or to the Boy Scout meetings. I would never play ball in Jefferson Park or on Randall's Island, where I lost a tooth.

I walked for hours on the Columbia University campus. I had never really seen it before. It was immense. I looked at every building and read every sign and studied every statue, especially a replica of Rodin's *The Thinker*, which was outside of Philosophy Hall. I saw the residence halls. Mine would be Hartley Hall. All freshmen had to stay there. I saw Van Am Quad and Hamilton Hall and John Jay, where the Lion's Den was. I saw it all and I felt as though I had landed on another planet, or perhaps had died and come back as another person.

From the steps in front of Low Memorial Library I saw the men in the NROTC (Naval Reserve Officers Training Corps) marching in formation. There was a V-12 program at Columbia, and a V-5 program for the Navy Air Force. If the war in the Pacific dragged on, I thought, I might join the Air Force program in order to stay in school. After all, I would be seventeen in September. When I told my friends, they thought I was crazy. "You mean like landing fighter planes on aircraft carriers?" said Weinberg.

"I guess so," I said, trying not to think about it realistically.

"What, are you crazy?"

I had seen some newsreels of the fighting on Okinawa, the bloodiest battle of the Pacific war, and all I could think of was to stay away from ground combat, landing craft and slaughter on the beaches, hand-to-hand fighting in trenches and through barbed wire. The Japanese were flushed out of bunkers with flame-throwers. They ran out on fire, screaming and burning to death. I could not imagine doing anything that violent. And then there were the Kamikazi pilots who flew their planes into our ships. I was haunted by the possibility of being drafted and considered declaring myself a conscientious objector. Then something terrible and wonderful happened.

I was very pleased with my summer job. Jeanne also had a job in Manhattan, and close enough for us to have lunch a few times a week. All I had to do was catch the subway at Broadway and 116th Street. She was only ten minutes away. We usually met at a cafeteria near the station. It was nice to see her that way, however briefly. A kiss hello, a kiss goodbye, and a sandwich in between with coke and conversation. Sometimes she'd come uptown and we would eat at the West End Deli, a real treat. Once in a while we were able to go to a movie at night. She had a friend who was willing to lie for her.

My job came with an old desk, my first. I felt very important, even though I was actually just the mail boy. The mail for the Admissions Office was dropped in my basket. There was a lot of it. I had to sort it, open it, and deliver it. In between, I was given some other clerical things to do. When they found out that I could type, I was given more work. They were impressed with me and I liked them. They were mostly women, some of whom had husbands in the military and were now wondering what would happen to them. Perhaps they would come home, perhaps they would wind up in the Pacific. The celebration of the European victory soon faded into dark speculations about how many American lives it would take to invade Japan. Some estimates ran up to half a million, if the Japanese chose to fight to the death.

When I did not meet Jeanne for lunch, I ate my sandwich on the stone bench outside of the Low Memorial Library, which had been replaced by the new library and was devoted now to office space. It was the classical centerpiece of the old campus, a circular and domed building that might have been designed in ancient Rome. I enjoyed sitting on the bench, because there was a pleasant view from there.

The long summer days came and went slowly. I was inching towards my new life. I saw my friends less often. I slept at home like a stranger. I slept on the day bed in the living room. There was a single bed in the back bedroom, which my brother used. In between there was a larger bedroom which was shared by my mother and sister. Nothing much had changed. These railroad flats were much the same. You had to walk through each room to get to the next. In the kitchen, under a yellow light, my mother and her cousin Guido still talked and sometimes argued. He smoked and read the newspaper. She cooked. At night he took the subway home to his mentally unstable wife. He still worked as an inspector of electrical repairs on the subway system, and still got through about two or three in the afternoon. Little by little I was separating myself from all that. I was eager to move out and to move on.

On a typical and quiet day in August, I took my lunch break on the stone bench and carried with me a copy of the *New York Times*. There was a front-page story about a new weapon, an atomic bomb, that was dropped on Hiroshima, causing extensive damage and loss of life. Details were not yet available from any source. No one in the office quite understood what it was all about. The terminology was odd. The whole thing was eerie and people talked about it in subdued voices, asking, "What's this about a new bomb?" And getting answers such as, "Just another bomb. They just keep getting bigger and bigger." I read every word in the newspaper but could not imagine anything new and revolutionary because I did not understand what *atomic power* meant. I don't think anybody really did, except those who made the thing.

I went back to work in the afternoon and overheard a few conversations. Some people had heard about the bomb, and some had not. There was speculation, but no hard information yet. It was the mystery surrounding the bomb and the terminology used to describe it that made people uneasy. By the time the office closed there were rumors circulating, about something devastating, something huge, something that might even end the war. Still, it was harde to imagine.

I went home and turned on the radio. As usual, my family were not especially interested. I listened over and over again to the reports as they came in. "The city of Hiroshima has been levelled," said one news broadcaster "Thousands of people have suffered severe burns." It must have been a large fire-bomb, I thought. But I was not satisfied. Something was happening. I could feel it in my whole body and in my mind.

Then some confirmation came, followed by enormous headlines. The real news was out. The nuclear bomb had destroyed most of a city of over 300,000 people in Japan. Everything was destroyed and deadly radiation was exposing survivors to lingering illness and death. It was an awesome weapon, controversial, dangerous. It could mean the end of war or the end of civilization. A mushroom cloud rose 20,000 feet over the city. A black cloud beneath it was full of ashes and debris. The terrible energy of the atom had been released by *fission*, another new word for most people. I didn't understand what *splitting* the atom meant. Lesko, who was well read, tried to explain it, but could not say how a *chain reaction* worked. We spent a few hours at the library, looking things up and arguing about whether or not this weapon would mean the war was over. Perhaps there would not have to be a bloody land invasion after all.

Two days later, one of these atomic bombs was dropped on Nagasaki, with dramatic results. Newpaper reports said that the bomb was equivalent to 20,000 tons of conventional explosives, about a thousand times more powerful than the largest bomb ever used. The world shuddered as the news spread. In a few more days the Japanese surrendered. The war was over.

We had just settled down for the long, hard invasion of Japan, when, in a flash, just two bombs put an end to the whole war. An awesome development that the public could not easily digest. Was it the judgement of God? Could it happen to us some day? Would America now rule the world?

It was terrible to discover that such weapons were possible, but I was relieved that we had made them before our enemies. And I was pleased for personal reasons. I would probably not be drafted. I would not have to go to war. And now I could begin my new life in a new world. I went forth with high hopes and great expectations.

Breinigsville, PA USA
08 January 2010
230275BV00006B/2/A